THE FUTURE-PROOF ARTIST:
Mastering The Five Staples of Music Industry Evolution

By Ryan J. Bruce

Copyright © 2024 RYAN BRUCE.

All rights reserved. No part of this publication may be reproduced, stored or transmitted in any form or by any means, electronic, mechanical, photocopying, recording, scanning, or otherwise without written permission from the publisher. It is illegal to copy this book, post it to a website, or distribute it by any other means without permission.

Ryan J. Bruce, herein referred to as "the author", asserts the moral right to be identified as the author of this work.

The author has no responsibility for the persistence or accuracy of URLs for external or third-party Internet Websites referred to in this publication and does not guarantee that any content on such Websites is, or will remain, accurate or appropriate.

Designations used by companies to distinguish their products are often claimed as trademarks. All brand names and product names used in this book and on its cover are trade names, service marks, trademarks and registered trademarks of their respective owners. The publishers and the book are not associated with any product or vendor mentioned in this book. None of the companies referenced within the book have endorsed the book.

First edition

DISCLAIMER

Please note that no individuals and entities mentioned in this book have provided the author with any form of compensation, consultation fees, or other incentives.

The analysis and commentary in this manuscript are solely a result of independent research by the author. The inclusion of all parties mentioned aims to provide a comprehensive industry overview, free from promotional or commercial bias.

'**THE FUTURE-PROOF ARTIST**: Mastering The Fives Staples of Music Industry Evolution

By Ryan J. Bruce.

ISBN/SKU: 979-8-3304-3253-0

www.thefutureproofartist.com

"The future belongs to those who prepare for it today."

- Malcolm X

TABLE OF CONTENTS

ABOUT THE AUTHOR	i
ACKNOWLEDGEMENTS	ii
PREFACE	v
INTRODUCTION	1
CHAPTER ONE: The Power of Community	8
CHAPTER TWO: The Art of Brand Strategy	23
CHAPTER THREE: Data is King	34
CHAPTER FOUR: Navigating Deals & The Law	53
CHAPTER FIVE: The Flow of Capital	67
CONCLUSION: A New Horizon	80
ENDNOTES	91
JOIN THE MOVEMENT	108

ABOUT THE AUTHOR

Ryan J. Bruce is a seasoned music business coach committed to helping artists understand the complexities of the recording industry. With over fifteen years of experience, Ryan has amassed extensive expertise in music marketing and business administration through his work with both major and independent labels and artists across genres. Understanding the unique challenges independent musicians face in building successful careers in today's landscape, he offers relevant resources and tailored coaching to help them navigate the music industry's dynamic trajectory.

Closely collaborating with his clients, Ryan has developed proven transformative strategies focused on helping independent artists build strong communities – the foundation for career success and longevity. His coaching techniques and resources have provided countless creatives with essential tools for penetrative marketing and overall career development.

Throughout his career, Ryan has worked with several acts who have gone on to achieve platinum certifications, GRAMMY nominations, and collaborate directly with some of the biggest names in music —including Beyoncé and Mariah Carey. Additionally, he has been featured in multiple publications such as HuffPost and Music Week.

ACKNOWLEDGMENTS

During the process of writing this book, I went back and forth in my mind on whether or not I should include an 'acknowledgments' page. I wondered if it was necessary, especially for this type of book. Plus, there are countless people I could mention who have been a part of my journey as a music industry professional. I was not sure where I would even start. But since we're here, let's rewind to the start (or, *my* start).

My very first encounter with the business of music came courtesy of the late Lucas Langdon, founder of a British independent urban music label named Awake Records. I met Lucas in my late teens, through a friend of mine that was pursuing a career as an artist. At the time, I had little to no knowledge of the recording industry, but my genuine love for music and general curious nature sparked a zealous desire to learn and absorb everything I could.

Acknowledging this, Lucas took me under his wing. I spent several years under his guidance and even hosted a daily show on an internet radio network he launched at the time. I could go on and share countless stories about my time working with Uncle Lucas, but the most valuable lesson I learned from him was the importance of passion and persistence. Those early experiences laid the foundation for everything I have done since, and continue to shape how I approach the music business today. Thank you, Lucas!

Another key person in my journey was Ms. Ruby Mulraine, whom I met at an industry networking event I was invited to attend at the Sony Music UK headquarters in 2013 (shoutout to Sam Potts and Remi Harris). After we connected, Ruby (a former executive producer for BBC Radio 1 and a founding producer for BBC Radio 1xtra), was kind enough to agree to be on a panel at my first industry conference.

I was an eager 22-year-old at the time and somehow was able to secure executives from companies like BMI, MTV, Columbia Records/Sony Music, INGrooves, and more for this event (which got coverage in Music Week and support from the British Phonographic Industry — BPI). Not bad for my first time!

Not only was Ruby one of the first speakers to say yes, she also spent time in countless mentorship sessions helping me map out my next steps (as an artist manager, at the time) and giving me some invaluable industry insights that opened my eyes to the power of strategic networking and cultivating relationships in this business. For that, I am forever indebted to you, Ruby! Thank you, kindly!

Lastly (and most importantly), my late mother, Yvonne. This 'acknowledgment' is, of course, a little more personal than the others. It also deviates from the pattern thus far of exclusively focusing on acknowledging key music industry professionals who have been an integral part of my journey.

Even though her professional career was outside of music, my mother was by far my biggest advocate. From catering my first industry conference at the last minute (after realizing I had no plans to feed anyone at an all-day event) to helping me structure and organize materials and resources for my clients, Mom's unwavering support extended far beyond these actions alone.

She was my sounding board, my voice of reason, and a source of endless encouragement. In moments of doubt or frustration (like the day before my first conference when I was considering canceling out of fear nobody would show up, though it ended up being packed to the brim) her belief in my potential never diminished. The work ethic and resilience I bring to my music industry career are a direct reflection of the values my mom instilled in me.

While she may not have been a 'music industry insider, her influence on my approach to this business and life, in general, is immeasurable. This book stands as a testament to her love, guidance, and the foundation she helped me build. I was, I am, and always will be… Yvonne's son.

All three of these individuals have played pivotal roles in my journey, yet still only represent a fraction of the many people who have influenced and supported me throughout my career. The music industry is built on relationships, and I've been fortunate to learn from and work alongside numerous talented professionals, mentors, and friends.

To those not mentioned by name here, please know that your impact on my personal and professional growth is not invalidated by this omission. Your guidance, support, and contributions have been invaluable in shaping my path and the insights shared in this book. I am deeply grateful for each interaction, collaboration, and learning opportunity that has brought me to this point.

This acknowledgment extends to all who have been part of my journey – your influence is woven into the fabric of my experiences and the knowledge I aim to share through this work.

PREFACE

In my years of working in the music industry, I've had the privilege of connecting with countless artists, executives, and other creative professionals, some of whom have shared with me their unique perspectives on what it takes to become successful. One particular question that has come up more than once in these conversations is the importance of having a clear 'why' — a driving purpose behind what you do.

It's a question I believe is critical, especially in a landscape where there's no shortage of 'how to' advice on building a career in music. Without a strong sense of 'why', it becomes all too easy to get 'lost in the noise' and lose sight of what truly matters to you. So, before we dive into the nuts and bolts of things, I want to take a moment to share my own 'why' and explain why I decided to write this book.

After years immersed in the business side of music, observing the changes and challenges faced by those pursuing a career in it (myself included), I realized we often found ourselves playing 'catch-up' to new technologies and trends. There was a constant pressure to adapt, but not always a clear roadmap for how to do so. As a consequence of my experience working with and for the 'big machines', I became inspired to equip independent music creators with the knowledge and tools necessary to not just survive but, more importantly, to thrive in this ever-evolving landscape. I wanted to help them build careers and legacies that are financially sustainable, impactful, and creatively fulfilling. This book is just another fruit of that inspiration, birthed out of a profound belief in the power of not just embracing change, but always being prepared for it.

As important as establishing the 'why', is explaining the 'what'. What does the title of this book actually mean, practically? What is it all about? And how is it helpful (if at all) to an artist who is feeling kinda 'lost in the sauce' and confused about the future? The answers to all these questions lie in the pages ahead, stemming from my observations and research of the immense impact of technology and cultural shifts in the music industry, dating back centuries. With each of these 'shifts', there are five pillars that have proven to be staples — and essentially form the foundation for success in this business. These pillars — community, brand strategy, data, deals & the law, and capital — intertwine to create a holistic approach to navigating the industry's moving landscape.

However, while each of those five aspects are critically important (as we'll explore in more detail later), this book goes beyond just the 'nuts and bolts' — it's an invitation to embark on an adventure of self-discovery and artistic growth, unbound by time. Through each page, I aim to empower you with knowledge, insights, and strategies that will elevate your creative pursuits and help you build a career that aligns with your vision and values, regardless of how the industry changes.

I am truly of the mindset that artists possess the power to shape the future of not just music itself, but the music business overall. So, whether you are a seasoned artist looking to elevate to even higher heights, or an aspiring talent just beginning your journey (or somewhere in between), let's embrace the next evolution of the music industry together. You are not just the future of music, you are the present — and if there was ever a time to chart your own course and create a legacy that transcends time, it's now.

With excitement,

Ryan J. Bruce

INTRODUCTION

Shaped by technological advances, legal frameworks, and cultural trends, the music industry has always been a complex and constantly evolving field. In my experience, five key elements have remained essential to achieving long-lasting success in this business for any artist. These are community, brand strategy, data, deals & the law, and capital. Since music became an industry, these five elements have been the foundational building blocks for a sustainable career. However, as the industry has evolved, the way these elements are applied has changed — and will continue to do so.

For example, the current dominance of social media and 'cyber communities' has made community-building even more of a crucial element for success and has allowed artists to meaningfully deepen their relationships with fans. Many fanbases have even adopted their own unique identities, such as Beyoncé's "Beyhive" or Taylor Swift's "Swifties" — something that was not as prevalent before the widespread use of online platforms. In a similar vein, the modern-day capabilities of data analytics have empowered artists and labels to facilitate more precise audience targeting, opening up new opportunities for growth.

Perhaps the most significant shifts in the industry over time have been the numerous introductions of revolutionary formats for music consumption over time — which, based on my observations, has happened roughly every 20 years since the early 1960s.

In 1963, Dutch tech company Philips introduced its first compact cassette recorder at the Funkausstellung Radio Exhibition in Berlin [1] — one of the most profound advancements in music technology that I believe has been overlooked. The cassette tape marked a new critical turning point, as fans were now empowered with greater control over how, when, and what music they consumed in a major way. With the new ability to create a more personalized experience, this 'control' gradually challenged the power of major record companies — a trend that persisted with subsequent music formats.

With cassette tapes, consumers could now duplicate and share music relatively easily. Remember trying to quickly capture your favorite song off the radio and copy it onto a cassette tape?! (or maybe that was just me). This newfound accessibility led to the emergence of the underground music scene in the mid-late 80s (from rising numbers of independent artists to consumers now starting to create personal playlists, and DJs introducing mixtape culture). With that opened up a whole new world of peer-to-peer music discovery, something that was previously at the exclusive discretion of the big record companies. Cassette players were also more portable than vinyl record players (the previous music format), allowing fans to listen to music 'on-demand' in their cars and on the go.

Around 20 years later, in 1982, the Compact Disc (CD), co-developed by Philips and Sony, first went into manufacturing [2]. Being thinner (thus easier to store) and containing significantly better audio quality, the CD quickly became the preferred format for music consumers — overtaking cassettes and vinyl. The convenience and control fans already had with cassettes were now amplified — particularly when Compact disc-recordables (CD-Rs) and CD burners became widely available and affordable.

However, almost another 20 years later, in 2001, music streaming services arose — becoming the ultimate paradigm shift. The very first on-demand streaming subscription service was Rhapsody (as part of listen.com) [3]. Within a few short years before and after Rhapsody's launch, other platforms like MP3.com, the first iteration of Napster, iTunes, and PeopleSound.com also launched and started to disrupt the scene, officially ushering us into "the digital age" of the music business.

The power (and potential) that this era gave to consumers was unprecedented. With immediate remote access to the world's largest music libraries for very affordable pricing, fans could now enjoy an unlimited and personalized music experience that was unparalleled, majorly surpassing what any prior form of music consumption could offer.

With that said, if you were to google the phrase "music streaming is the future" right now, you'd likely be met with a ton of think pieces justifying this statement — despite the format already being over two decades old. Whether they are talking about the potential for more revenue streams down the line, or unpacking the capabilities of predicting trends using data, the general idea amongst many is that 'this is it' — we've reached the 'destination'. However, if streaming in its current form is what is dominating now, and has been for some years, there remains a possibility for history to repeat itself, potentially leaving room for a new major innovation to emerge and revolutionize the market in the future.

Traditional streaming might seem like the 'final destination' when it comes to how we consume music, but with the continued growth of physical formats like vinyl continuing to post year-over-year growth, there are bound to be jagged edges in the music consumption landscape [10]. Though streaming has radically reshaped the business, the recent rise in the value of physical music speaks to some consumers' ongoing need for a more direct and traditional connection with their favorite songs. This trend suggests that the future of how people are consuming music may not be a one-size-fits-all approach (as it has been in many ways), but a much more sophisticated and multifaceted environment that caters to a range of listening behaviors and experiences.

Based on the timeline of my theory laid out above, we are a little over 20 years from the initial introduction of streaming (2001). Thus, we could now be on the verge of yet another major evolution in music consumption that will likely, again, give consumers a groundbreaking level of connection and control over their experience with recorded (and possibly even live) music.

This time, it's fair to assume that the evolution could be led or influenced by the convergence of Web3 (the next generation of the internet), AI, and the metaverse — a development that will likely co-exist with Web2 technologies, like streaming, for years to come.

The 'metaverse' is a *developing* Web3 virtual space where people can interact with each other and with digital objects in a highly immersive manner. Combined with the power and future development of AI, this has the potential to revolutionize the music industry in ways we can't yet even fathom. I mean, imagine a future where fans can not only stream their favorite albums but also explore immersive, AI-generated worlds that visually and sonically respond to the music, creating a unique and personalized experience for each listener.

As incomprehensible as anything beyond streaming in its current form might sound, it sounds just as incomprehensible now that, according to a 1983 BBC News report, EMI (the UK's largest record company at the time) resisted the concept of CDs when they first launched, likely because they could not envision a future beyond cassette tapes and vinyl records at the time. Ironically, the same company also resisted Vinyl LPs when they first launched, as they were unsure whether or not the format was here to say [4].

Subsequently, in 2007 (four years after the launch of iTunes), EMI's then-Chairman, Guy Hands, had likely learned from the music giant's past mistakes and allegedly told staffers that the company must "embrace digital or die" in a leaked memo [9], underscoring the criticality of evolving to avoid becoming irrelevant. This speaks to the music industry's long history of being slow to get ahead of new technologies and business models — though that has certainly changed in recent times (more on this later).

At first, labels struggled to get a handle on the digital age, and, as a result, found themselves getting the short end of the stick in some cases. For instance, when Apple unveiled the iTunes Store in 2003, the California-based tech company quickly ended up controlling a significant portion of the music industry, even though they had no prior involvement in the business of music. By July 2004, the iTunes Store had sold 100 million songs — solidifying its position as a true power player [5].

Despite this success, iTunes was met with mixed feelings across the industry. Even though the major labels agreed to license their content to iTunes, many felt the concept was a threat to the 'album' and recorded music revenue as a consequence. For example, back when artist and label executive Jay Z initially dropped his "American Gangster" album in 2007 (during his time as President & CEO of Def Jam Recordings), he refused to release it to iTunes [6]. He stated, *"As movies are not sold scene by scene, this collection will not be sold as individual singles"*.

Not only did the Roc Nation founder end up releasing the album to iTunes (four years later in 2011), he then went on to fully embrace the current reality of the digital era by launching his own streaming service, 'TIDAL', just three years after, in 2014. At this point, consumers accessing individual tracks was the norm and, for most artists and recorded music rights holders, could no longer be avoided.

This is just one example of how despite having valid concerns about the future of digital, the industry failed to get ahead of the curve and lost control of its own distribution channels — though they later worked to somewhat regain them via equity deals with digital service providers such as Spotify, Soundcloud, and Vevo [7].

Ironically, though, the same thing is happening once again. In a 2022 op-ed for Music Business Worldwide, Deborah Mannis-Gardner, President of DMG Clearances, stated that *"the music industry is playing catch-up to the world of Web3 and the rapid pace with which it is changing and growing."* [8]

While the shape of the industry's future may be unknown, one thing is clear: the music industry must remain open to innovation and be willing to embrace new technologies and formats that can enhance and deepen the connection between artists and fans. Through understanding and catering to the diverse preferences and desires of music lovers, from the analog warmth of vinyl to the boundless possibilities of the digital frontier, both artists and labels can better position themselves for success in an increasingly complex and dynamic business.

In this book, we will lay out what I believe is the blueprint for avoiding the old habit of playing catch-up in the future from an artist's perspective, and provide insights on how you as a music creator can confidently chart your own course — essentially making you a 'future-proof artist'. A lot can be said about the ins and outs of this business. However, I assure you that, for artists, all of it will somehow root back to one (or more) of the five staples we're about to dive into, starting with what I believe is the most important of them all: Community.

CHAPTER 1:
The Power of Community

Allow me to begin by challenging everything you may have thought you knew about the music industry... Music was not created to be sold!

To further unpack this, let's take it back to the very beginning.

Long before music evolved into the multi-billion dollar industry it is today, music was simply a creative expression that was experienced by individuals and communities. While it is difficult to pinpoint the exact time and place where music first occurred, some of the earliest recorded examples of people gathering for musical performances date back to Ancient Egypt. According to the University of Michigan's Kelsey Museum of Archeology, there is evidence of live music and instruments existing as early as 3,100 BCE. [11]

In more recent history, the first known recording of a live music performance was by the French inventor Édouard-Léon Scott de Martinville in 1860, who used a device called the phonautograph to capture sound waves on paper — as corroborated by Time Magazine and The History Channel [12]. This took place 17 years prior to the invention of Thomas

Edison's 'phonograph' (a device still seen around the world today in the form of the Grammy Award statue). [13]

With each new advancement in music, from live performances to music publishing to recorded music, more and more people started galvanizing around it, creating communities and making it an integral part of their culture. This communal aspect of music has been a constant throughout history, as highlighted by best-selling author Bernard Marr in an article for Forbes who stated *"Music has always been about social activities and coming together"*. [14]

The development of communities around music (assisted by the technological advancements that facilitated this experience) was essentially what shifted music from just a creative expression to a profitable commodity. This evolution, however, is not unique to the business side of music. The same concept also holds true for artists or creative individuals.

In the same way that community is what transformed music into a sustainable industry, building communities of their own is what allows artists to have sustainable careers. While talent is still arguably important, the success of today's artists is less about that talent and more about that artist's audience.

Without an audience, talent cannot be monetized, and without monetization, music has no business value, labels have no capital, and ultimately artists have no careers. Through establishing their own communities (or 'fan bases'), artists and labels are then able to sell records, book paid shows, and land economically sustaining deals that raise their profiles and enrich their industry status.

One of the benefits of today's landscape is that (with the help of social media and other tools) creators now have more direct access to consumers. Prior to this, avenues needed to reach consumers — such as radio, television, and conventional marketing channels — were some of the exclusive benefits of signing to record labels. This was due to the significant financial resources and accessibility necessary to utilize said channels.

Record labels playing the 'middleman' was (and still is) highly successful in many cases, and introduced the world to the biggest artists in history. On the other hand, this created a sole reliance on those record companies to build, connect, and grow an artist's community. In the earlier days of the music business, without the support of a label, it was very difficult (if not impossible) for an artist to communicate with the outside world — thus making it almost impossible to achieve commercial success, even for the most esteemed artists. A good example is Prince.

Prince, like many artists, had a somewhat complex relationship with major labels. Throughout his career, he expressed disdain for the dynamics between himself and his then-label Warner Music Group and what he felt was the mistreatment of artists across the board by record companies in general. In the early 90s, Prince had a disagreement with Warner over their reluctance to release his extensive collection of music on a more frequent schedule. He responded to their resistance by adopting an unpronounceable stage name known as the "Love Symbol", since Warner had trademarked the name 'Prince'. During this period, he was referred to as either "the Artist" or "the Artist Formerly Known as Prince", making it somewhat difficult for Warner to market his releases. [15]

Withstanding, as much as Prince was not always a fan of major labels, his biggest successes depended on them — and the proof is in the pudding. Prince's biggest-selling album was (and still is) 'Purple Rain', released in 1984 by Warner Bros. Records.

CHAPTER 1: THE POWER OF COMMUNITY

The release peaked at #1 on the Billboard 200 chart, went 13x platinum in the US (thereby achieving diamond status), and has sold over 25 million copies worldwide [16]. On the contrary, every single Prince album that failed to chart on the Billboard 200 whatsoever, including '20Ten' (2010), 'One Night Alone…' (2002), and 'The Chocolate Invasion' (2004), were all albums he released independently — without any major label-backing.

This demonstrates one of the problems that used to occur for commercial artists. If their relationship with major record companies halted or ended altogether, they often struggled to maintain a connection with their community — leading many to believe they had "fallen off". Statements like "that artist isn't as big as they used to be" were (and still are) often said to that effect — when in actuality, what that more than likely meant was 'said artist' does not have as big of a marketing budget as they used to (due to independent financing). Because of this, much of their community was not "hearing" from them.

Today, that has changed. Artists can directly cultivate and nurture their own audiences, thereby increasing their worth and leverage — as opposed to relying on a label to build a base for them. One unique case study of an independent artist who built their own community from the ground up is the late Nipsey Hussle, who sadly passed away in 2019.

Nipsey was a rapper and entrepreneur from the Crenshaw district of Los Angeles who founded his own record label, 'All Money In No Money Out', and started out releasing his music completely independently — often making references to it in his lyrics. In the song "Last Time I Checc'd", Nipsey rapped: *"No co-sign, I ain't need radio to do mine, I done fine"* [17]. The single was the second to be promoted from Nipsey's debut (and only) album 'Victory Lap' (released via a licensing deal with Warner

Music Group's Atlantic Records, after 13 years of releasing mostly independent material and building his audience). The album was a moderate success, landing a top five debut on the Billboard 200, and achieving a Grammy nomination for 'Best Rap Album' — all prior to Nipsey's passing. [18]

One technique Nipsey used was building a strong sense of community within his local neighborhood. On top of opening 'The Marathon Clothing' store in South Central Los Angeles, where he sold his own line of merchandise, Nipsey also invested in local businesses such as Vector90 (a co-working space in Crenshaw for budding entrepreneurs), a fish market, barbershop, and multiple restaurants [19] [20].

These investments were more than just savvy business moves; they were a manifestation of Nipsey's deep-rooted belief in the value of economic self-sufficiency and community empowerment, expressed in his music. By providing resources and opportunities for his neighbors to thrive, he not only uplifted his immediate surroundings but also inspired others in the wider community to follow in his footsteps. Nipsey's actions aligned with (and often spoke louder) than his words, which allowed his audience to recognize the true sincerity behind his message.

This authenticity and dedication to his community gave Nipsey a unique brand identity that resonated strongly with like-minded demographics. His message of grassroots entrepreneurship and economic empowerment became an integral part of his artistic persona, setting him apart from other rappers in the industry. Whether intentional or not, the practical alignment between his values and his brand strategy proved to be a powerful combination that fueled his success both as a musician and a community leader (more on that in the next chapter).

The examples of Prince and Nipsey Hussle's ability to connect with their audience and the inherent complexities it entails present us with an array of valuable insight, while equally giving rise to a universal challenge. That challenge being 'How does the average independent artist, perhaps juggling a full or part-time job (and/or other responsibilities), achieve all of this in the face of an industry where 100,000 new songs are being released every day?' [21]

To answer this, we have to discover the formula here. What has been the commonality of building community in each major evolution of music?

As we covered in the introduction, each evolution gradually gave consumers more power to tailor their recorded music experience, thereby enabling artists to form deeper connections with their communities.

Not only have these evolutions changed consumer behavior but, unaware to some, they have also had a monumental impact on the creative process itself. The relationship between the costs of distribution, the constraints of hardware, and the creative expression of musicians has been somewhat of an implicit tussle since the music industry began. This constant 'push and pull' has subconsciously shaped the approach musicians take to create music and, as a consequence, how listeners consume it.

Back in 2014, I was speaking at a music business conference in the UK for an independent industry body. During my presentation, I asked attendees why they thought the average song length is (or was) usually somewhere around 3-5 minutes. The most common answers were "radio" (referring to the time limits of broadcasting) and "consumer attention spans". While these are very fair and arguably accurate assumptions, in actuality, the length of a song has a lot more to do with the physical constraints of phonograph records that dictated the length (and structure) of songs in the early days of recorded music.

The 78 rpm phonograph shellac record, most popular during the late 1800s and mid-1900s, could only hold about 2-5 minutes of audio per side, depending on the size of the disc (the 12-inch held the maximum amount of playing time) [23]. This meant artists had to confine their compositions to this time frame. As a result, the 3-5 minute song was adopted as the norm and became ingrained in the collective consciousness of both artists and listeners.

One of the formats that followed the 78 rpm (revolutions/spins per minute) phonograph record was the 33 ⅓ rpm vinyl LP introduced by Columbia Records in 1948. A year later, in 1949, came the 45 rpm vinyl (with the 7-inch version becoming the standard for singles). Then, fourteen years later in 1963, came the Philips cassette tape (covered in the introduction).

This marked a significant shift, offering artists more creative freedom, with the 12-inch 33 ⅓ rpm vinyl LP providing an unprecedented 44 minutes of total recording time (22 minutes per side) and the earliest cassette tapes allowing up to 60 minutes of total recording time (30 minutes per side) [24] [25]. This opened the door for longer-form compositions and more experimental song structures, as evidenced by recordings such as Jimi Hendrix's "Voodoo Child" (a track released in 1968, just under 15 minutes in total length) — something that wouldn't have been possible prior to 1948.

Skip ahead to the digital era and the restrictions of physical mediums have erased. With streaming platforms and digital distribution, an album can essentially contain as many songs

CHAPTER 1: THE POWER OF COMMUNITY

as an artist desires, and a single track can stretch on for hours — such as Singaporean artist yeule's "The Things They Do For Love" (a track with over 4 hours running time).

Yet this infinite world of creative possibility is, in a way, just as restrictive. Rather than being defined by the limitations of physical formats that indirectly controlled musical creativity in previous eras, much of today's creativity (and its success) is now shaped by the unique characteristics of the digital music ecosystem.

Platforms like Spotify, which have become essential for artists to reach and engage with global music fans, have introduced new factors that equally impact the creative process in ways many artists may not even be aware of. One of the most influential factors in this new landscape is the significance of a song's first 30 seconds.

Most streaming platforms, including Spotify, Apple Music, and YouTube, require a song to be consumed for at least 30 seconds to count as one 'stream'. Anything less and the rights holders do not get paid. Additionally, if a song gets added to a Spotify playlist, one of its algorithms takes note of how long (past the initial 30 seconds) consumers continue to listen to the song. This is called the 'retention rate'.

If Spotify notices a song's retention rate is particularly high, it will not only get added to more of their curated playlists, but it will also appear in 'personalized playlists' for more and more people over time — potentially enlarging the artist's audience. This speaks to the reason why the average song running time on the Billboard Hot 100 Chart has decreased from 4:14 in the 1990s to 3:15 in the 2020s [26]. The shorter the song, the easier it is to achieve a 'high' retention rate, keep attention spans, and, thus, reach a wider audience — impacting the growth of your community.

For example, if a song's running time is 3:15 (the average length of a song in the 2020s), only a little over 2 minutes of listening is needed to achieve a 70% retention rate. But if a song's running time is 4:14 (the average song length in the 90s), 2 minutes of listening will only give a 45% retention rate. This is important to know because a report by music analyst Paul Lamere for musicmachinery.com found that almost 50% of Spotify listeners will skip a track before it finishes — and 35% skip in the first 30 seconds (meaning that will not even count towards the artist's or right holder's streams and revenue).[27]

One of the other main reasons why songs have decreased in length is due to streaming economics. Whether a song's running time is 3:15 or 4:14, the artist and/or rights holders generate the same royalty rate per stream. And with retention rates being what they are, it could (in some cases) be more beneficial to have 2 songs with a running time of around 2:07 (for example) than one song with a running time of 4:14. This can potentially expand your reach (and community) as an artist, as well as increasing your revenue.

With algorithms that appear to favor certain track lengths and credit structures, artists now have new things to consider when crafting their music to maximize its potential for success on digital platforms and reach the right audience, building up their community.

In noting all of this, it's equally (or arguably more) important to stay true to your artistic vision while also being aware of the mechanics of streaming platforms and the preferences of modern listeners so you can effectively strike a balance between creativity and the realities of the modern music industry.

As a developing artist, you may not have the freedom of time or capital to invest in local businesses like Nipsey Hussle or have the financial backing of Warner Bros. Records like Prince, but what you do have is the ability to take advantage of the current (and future landscape) to implement the same principles (as the ones above) that continuously strengthen ties with your audience.

On that note, we cannot talk about community without doing a dive into a concept that's been buzzing in the music industry lately — superfans. Don't mistake this for just another industry buzzword. There is solid data backing up why you should care about these dedicated supporters and nurture your relationships with them.

According to a 2023 Luminate study, about 15% of the U.S. population over age 13 fall into the 'superfan' category [28]. Meaning, if you have 10,000 active fans (which you can define as the average number of people that engage with your music every month and may occasionally buy tickets to a show), you should have a goal of achieving at least 1,500 superfans. And, with something like a $10 per month Patreon community with the right strategy, those 1,500 superfans could significantly increase your income.

As a quick note, it is important to separate fans from followers. 10,000 Instagram or TikTok followers does not mean you have 10,000 actual fans. 'Fans' are those who frequently consume your music, but usually in ways that require minimal commitment in terms of time, money, and effort. The concept of superfans goes way beyond that. But, what exactly are they, specifically?

Superfans are not the average listeners who might stream your new single just a few times. We're talking about the folks who 'live and breathe' your music, your brand, and your story.

Luminate defines this subset as consumers that engage with an artist in at least five different ways (e.g. streaming their catalog, engaging with them on social media, attending live shows, purchasing merchandise, subscribing to their newsletter, etc). Thus, one of the reasons you may be struggling to foster a superfan community is because you may have limited offerings, suited mostly to casual listeners. Simply having active social media accounts and your music on streaming platforms might be one of the barriers stopping you from monetizing and connecting with the most dedicated fans among your audience.

While they represent a relatively small number of your fan base, superfans are the ones who feel a deep personal connection to you as an artist. Your music isn't just something they listen to; it's part of who they are. Additionally, these consumers are often the tastemakers in their social circles by being the first to discover new tracks and most likely to share them with family and friends. And perhaps most importantly, they're the glue that holds your artist community together, building connections with other fans and creating a sense of belonging around your music.

Now, you might be thinking, "That's great, is building a superfan community really worth it?" Well, the data makes it pretty clear. One of Luminate's 2023 reports shared that superfans spend a whopping 80% more on music categories than the average listener (in the U.S.). They are not just streaming; they're those 'repeat customers' who are consistently buying physical albums, merchandise, and showing up to gigs. In fact, the Luminate study found that physical music buyers are more than twice as likely to be superfans compared to the average listener.

But let's be clear — the value of superfans goes way beyond

just dollars and cents. These are also your grassroots marketing team and brand ambassadors, which can make all the difference to independent artists without a large team (or much of one at all). They're the ones creating fan art, running fan pages, and starting conversations about your music on social media. In essence, they're amplifying your reach in ways that traditional marketing often can't touch.

And, you might be thinking, "I'm a 'small artist' and don't have much of a fan base at all, never mind superfans". But, if you remain consistent with releasing content that properly represents your brand, you will likely start to identify individuals who (for example) consistently engage with your content on social media. Those are the ones you need to start building bonds with.

But, how exactly do you build those bonds? Here are a few strategies to consider:

1. **Exclusive Content**: If you identify people who have consistently supported you, give them a 'backstage pass' to your creative process. Early previews of new tracks, behind-the-scenes footage, or special edition merch can make them feel like true insiders.
2. **Direct Engagement**: Interact with them on social media, host live Q&A sessions, or set up casual meet-and-greets (no matter how small). Remember, they mostly desire that personal connection.
3. **Community Building**: Once you notice your community starts growing, create spaces where they can connect with each other. This could be anything from a dedicated social media channel to hangouts before or after a show.
4. **Show Appreciation**: Acknowledge their support. A

shoutout on social media or during a live show can go a long way.

Understanding and nurturing your superfan base is no longer just a nice-to-have — it's becoming essential for building a sustainable career as an independent artist. In an industry where standing out is increasingly challenging, fostering a superfan subset of your community could be the key to cutting through the noise and creating a lasting impact that survives any major shift.

Looking ahead, it's clear that the pace of technological change in the music industry will only continue to accelerate, presenting both challenges and opportunities. But rather than getting caught up in the specifics of each new platform or trend, you should instead remain focused on the fundamental human desires that drive your connection with fans: the desire for belonging, self-expression, and shared experiences. Keeping these timeless values at the forefront of your pursuit and being willing to experiment and take risks will put you in a position to better navigate the unpredictable dynamics of the future with both confidence and purpose.

Ultimately, the power to build and sustain a thriving community lies not in any particular technology or tactic, but in the authenticity, creativity, and resilience of you as an artist. Central to this is having the courage to be vulnerable, share your truth in creative ways, and invite fans into your world in a way that feels genuine and meaningful. Whether through music, merchandise, live performances, virtual experiences, or beyond, the goal should always be to create a sense of connection and belonging that transcends the medium.

It is yet to be determined how the next wave of the industry will unfold. Will AI and the metaverse have a major impact on the music business? Or will it simply end up being a small complimentary add-on to what already exists? Either way, what we do know is that major changes of some sort are inevitable. However, the exact details of what those changes will look like are not nearly as important as the underlying principles thereof — particularly that which applies to independent artists.

On a 2023 episode of 'The View', the panel discussed AI, talking about the concept of 'CarynAI' — an AI chatbot launched by Snapchat influencer Caryn Marjorie in partnership with tech startup Forever Voices. The highly intelligent chatbot is based on over 2000 hours of designing and coding using Marjorie's voice, personality, and behaviors. With this, paying 'clients' can have their own unique relationship with 'Caryn' via her AI persona [22].

Considering the inherent challenge for itinerant artists to personally connect with each and every one of their fans around the world, it becomes a lot easier to envision such transformative technology potentially being fully embraced by the music industry at large in the future. Not to mention it falls right in line with the idea proposed above regarding each evolution creating a more personal experience and deeper 'connection' with fans.

If building authentic connections remains your priority as an artist, you will always have a solid springboard for your music — with or without major backing. How you decide to go about this, however, will be heavily dependent upon how you wish to be perceived. Do you 'have' to take advantage of every single channel available, past and present, to build/engage your community? Or should you instead focus your energy on specific areas? Much of this brings us to our next chapter, being brand strategy.

CHAPTER 2:
The Art of Brand Strategy

In my initial consultation meetings with independent labels, I usually always ask one critical question; 'What is your biggest current challenge?'. The response I hear most often is typically something to the effect of 'cutting through the noise' (referring to market saturation).

With AI and other future technologies evolving to make music creation and distribution even more accessible and streamlined, market saturation is only poised to continue intensifying. With this in mind, one of the best ways to ensure you distinguish yourself from the masses is not just by creating an artist brand, but by the continuous implementation of an effective brand *strategy*. But, what exactly is that? And how does it apply to independent recording artists today *and* in the future?

Simply put, a brand strategy is the process of defining and communicating an individual/entity's values, mission, and unique selling proposition. It involves understanding your audience, analyzing the market, and developing both a clear and consistent brand image and message across all of your communication channels (i.e. your music/content, website, social media, in-person appearances, and other mediums). Think of a brand as the embodiment of what a person or entity represents, while the brand strategy pertains to the means of conveying what that is.

For an independent artist without the backing of a 'big machine', the importance of a strong brand strategy cannot be overstated — and is essential in the process of building a community. Without a well-defined brand and brand strategy, artists risk blending in with the masses and being easily forgotten by their audience (or simply struggling to even build one) — thereby increasing the pressure of having to consistently release hit records or viral content due to the fact that their audience has nothing else to connect with outside of just their music.

While achieving viral moments and hit records can be necessary and certainly fuels an artist's growth, this is often unpredictable and very difficult to control — especially for independent creators. Furthermore, too much of a focus on those particular 'success metrics' may inadvertently steer artists exclusively towards chasing algorithms at the expense of authentic engagement — although comprehending the significance of both is essential (more on algorithms later). This is just one of the reasons why even established artists have diversified their endeavors — engaging in other forms of media such as podcasting, brand partnerships, books, speaking engagements, entrepreneurship, and beyond.

The importance of this diversification partially relates to the fact that, according to Variety, over 100,000 new songs are uploaded to digital service providers (i.e. Spotify, Apple Music) every day — as we mentioned in the previous chapter. Think about that. That means if you release a song today, within just 30 days of its release, 3 million new songs have been released attempting to capture the attention of music fans. The more alarming statistic, though, is that in 2023 an estimated 45 million songs received *zero* plays on Spotify alone — as reported by Music Business Worldwide. [29]

Aside from what may be limited marketing dollars and other contributing factors, one of the major components here is likely the lack of a unique brand strategy. With this extreme competition in today's music industry (which is still largely dominated by the major labels) artists who are simply continuing to just release music, without identifying their audience by creating a brand strategy, will have a difficult time picking up and retaining new listeners.

It is important to note, though, that branding and brand strategies are not intended to confine performers to a rigid framework but rather to establish a distinctive identity. The key to achieving this lies in carefully crafting and executing a specific brand identity narrative, which enables artists to effectively communicate their individuality and establish a strong connection with their audience.

A brief example we can revisit is Nipsey Hussle, who we mentioned earlier. Nipsey is not just known for his music, but he is also widely known for his values (social entrepreneurship, giving back to local communities, and providing opportunities). His particular approach highlights the importance of defining what you stand for, which brings us to one of the easiest ways to start working on your artist brand strategy. Ask yourself the following: 'What do I want people to think and how do I want them to feel when they encounter me or consume my content?' Empowered? Encouraged? Nostalgic? Energized?. In other words, what *emotions* do you want to tap into? Once you've answered that, the next step is to drill down and get as *specific* as possible — ensuring that what you are outlining authentically represents who you actually are as a person. From there, you'll be on your way to better defining yourself, your artistry, and how you can identify, develop, and impact your community.

These insights essentially become the root of every single you release, every album title you select, and ultimately every strategic move you make. This can be seen in Adele's album title strategy, "19," "21," "25," and "30", all named after her age when she recorded and/or released them, while Ed Sheeran has consistently used mathematical symbols for his album titles [30] [31]. This is all a form of branding, which can also inform the artwork you select, the shows you perform, the deals you secure, your marketing campaigns, and more.

On the topic of marketing, it is critically important to understand the fundamental contrast between the meaning of marketing and the objective of branding. While branding is the process of establishing a unique and distinguishable identity to create an emotional connection with your audience, marketing (on the other hand) involves promoting, advertising, and selling to that audience. For example, Beyonce's decision to refrain from frequent media interviews in recent years has become a core part of her brand, whereas her 2024 Super Bowl commercial with Verizon announcing her new music and subsequent new album via social media serves as more of a *marketing* tactic. [32]

To put it simply, an artist's brand serves as the foundation that fuels the success of their marketing efforts — much like how a seed provides the essential health and nourishment for the growth of its contents. Many times, we put a huge emphasis on the importance of marketing — and, while it is essential, the more time you dedicate to strengthening your brand identity, the easier and more effortless it becomes to promote your projects and effectively expand your reach.

One of the secrets of effective branding relates to something we touched on earlier: the concept of emotional branding. How do you want people to *feel* when they encounter you?! This is an old-age strategy that has been used in various industries for decades, and the music business is no exception. Legendary artists like The Beatles, Elvis Presley, and Michael Jackson did not just connect with fans by releasing music — they also, intentionally or unintentionally, used 'emotional branding' to catapult them into unprecedented levels of success.

If you were to reflect specifically on Michael Jackson's emotional branding strategy, for example, you would find he often used six specific methods:

Empathy Through Art

One of the most significant and foundational ways Michael Jackson connected to the emotions of his audience was through his music. Michael's songs would explore universal themes of love, compassion, as well as social issues. Global hits like "Heal the World", "Man in the Mirror", and "We Are The World", inspired listeners to reflect on making a positive change, creating a sense of shared empathy and responsibility that many of us could connect with.

Vulnerability

In interviews and documentaries, Jackson would open up about some of his lifelong struggles, allowing fans to relate to him on a personal level. He spoke candidly about his childhood experiences (or lack thereof), shyness offstage, and the mounting pressure of fame [33]. Though much of the general public does not share those experiences, the authenticity displayed in sharing them 'humanized' Michael to many — making him more relatable and seemingly more approachable, ultimately deepening his emotional connection with his audience.

Empathy Through Art

To millions, if not billions, around the world, Michael Jackson's electrifying performances were undeniable, and were a testament to his ability to evoke strong emotions. His energy and choreography, like the iconic 'moonwalk', conveyed an unparalleled passion and dedication to his craft.

Fans were electrified by Michael's stage presence, which created an emotional connection through the power of his artistry. It was a common part of Jackson's stage routine to stand completely still for extended periods of time (like the start of his 1993 Super Bowl Halftime Performance), building the crowd's anticipation for his next move — stirring intense feelings of emotion in the process. This is something more recent artists like Beyoncé, Usher, and Chris Brown have frequently emulated — because, well, it works!

Humanitarian Efforts

Michael Jackson had a strong commitment to humanitarian causes throughout his lifetime. He was actively involved in various charitable endeavors, supporting children's hospitals, disaster relief efforts, and education initiatives, which led to him being honored with the Presidential Public Safety Commendation by President Ronald Reagan in 1984 [34]. This dedication to 'making the world a better place' further resonated with his audience, just as his music did. These efforts made Jackson 'believable' — as it demonstrated that his music was truly a reflection of his real-life values.

Fan Engagement

Jackson engaged with his fans in very meaningful ways, despite the time restraints that came with being one of the most famous celebrities on the planet. He regularly visited sick fans in the hospital [35] and even invited some to his home for special events in partnership with the Make-A-Wish Foundation [36]. These interactions naturally made fans feel valued and appreciated, strengthening the emotional connection they had with the pop star.

Now, I know you are probably thinking that Michael's ability to do some of the above was due to his status and profile, which reached a level that even some of today's top artists can only dream of. And yes, while it's true that Michael Jackson was a global superstar with substantial resources at his disposal, independent artists on the come-up can still apply some of the strategies he used to create emotional branding in their own unique ways by crafting relatable content (not just music) that speaks to universal experiences and emotions.

While Michael Jackson's strategies may seem out of reach for the average independent artist, the core principles can be adapted at any level. Here are just a few examples of how emerging artists can create their own emotional brand connection:

Authenticity Through Art

Leverage your own unique perspectives to create music that resonates on a personal level. Instead of aiming for global anthems, focus on honest storytelling that reflects your experiences and those of your immediate community. A song about struggling to make rent, or even navigating a creative field as an independent in the digital age can be just as powerful as "Heal the World" to the right audience.

Strategic Vulnerability

In the age of social media, independent artists have unprecedented access to their current and potential audience. Use this to your advantage by sharing your journey — the ups and downs, the creative process, and the challenges you face. This doesn't mean oversharing; rather, it's about curating moments of vulnerability that align with your brand and values. A behind-the-scenes video of your songwriting process or a candid post about overcoming writer's block could create a sense of connection and reliability.

Memorable Live Performances

While you may not be performing at the Super Bowl, every show is an opportunity to create a lasting impression. Develop a signature element in your performance — whether it's an interactive moment with the audience, a unique consistent stage setup, or a memorable opening sequence. Remember, in the age of social media, even a small club show can reach a global audience if it's captivating enough to be shared.

Community Involvement

You don't need to establish a global foundation to make an impact. Start local. Participate in community events, support local causes, or offer your talents to fundraisers. This not only helps build your reputation but also creates genuine connections within your community. As Nipsey Hussle demonstrated, community involvement can be a powerful pillar of your brand.

Intimate Fan Engagement

Visiting sick fans in hospitals might not be applicable for you, but there are so many other ways to create meaningful interactions with your fans. Hosting intimate listening parties, responding personally to messages, or creating a digital fan club with exclusive content. In the digital age, tools like Patreon allow artists to create close-knit communities around their music.

Consistent Visual Identity

Developing a cohesive visual aesthetic across all your platforms can be very impactful. This doesn't require a big budget — consistency in color schemes, typography, and imagery style can go a long way. It's important that your album artwork, social media posts, and stage design all feel part of the same visual universe.

Value Driven Messaging

Align your brand with values that genuinely matter to you. This could be anything from environmental sustainability to mental health awareness. Weave these themes into your music, your social media presence, and your interactions with fans. This gives your audience something to connect with beyond just the music.

The goal ought not be to try and replicate Michael Jackson's (or anyone else's) career, but to apply similar branding principles in a way that is authentic to you and feasible within your means. In today's fragmented music landscape, building a dedicated niche following through emotional branding can be more valuable (and attainable) than chasing mass appeal, particularly if you are independent with limited resources. This more focused approach is what creates the kind of loyalty that sustains long-term careers.

In today's industry, much of the above can be efficiently accomplished by understanding the power of data analytics. Data is what provides artists with unprecedented insights into their community's preferences, behaviors, and, if studied more intricately, their emotions. Through harnessing the true power of data, artists can not only understand their position in the market, but they can also learn more about what resonates with their community on an emotional level, and thus, further lean into it.

One of the multiple ways this can be done is by using sentiment analysis tools — which allow you to analyze the emotional tone of mass digital text (comments, online chatter) in bulk. From there, you can gain insight into how your audience feels about you/your content in one place, and even identify common keywords that provide clues about what aspects of your content are connecting with them.

This is a great way to lead us into the next chapter, which, as you likely guessed, extensively explores the world of data — uncovering some of its history, and how artists can utilize data to bond with their community on a deeper level.

CHAPTER 3:
Data is King

Data is merely information — something that has always been necessary for growth in the music industry. Whether it was manually keeping track of sales from sheet music and vinyl records, monitoring which cities sold the most concert tickets, the songs that were receiving the most radio spins, conducting consumer behavior surveys, tracking performance royalties, or anything else, data has been essential to understanding the market.

Today, like any other industry that utilizes technology, the level of data available in the music business has catapulted to unprecedented levels, ranging from overly detailed DSP (digital service provider, e.g. Spotify) analytics to extreme targeting using digital ads.

Over time, this data has become more and more specific, giving a much deeper insight into consumer behavior, interests, and preferences that go beyond simply informing you of the most profitable cities to tour or what radio stations are playing your records most often. Leveraging such advanced data allows both artists and labels to make more informed decisions about their next moves. However, more important than access to data, is the analysis of it.

In a meeting with a major label VP of Strategy some years

ago, one of the things he shared was that while data has become more refined, if we do not understand how to properly examine and apply it, it renders itself somewhat useless. The point being, regardless of how much data is available to you, its value is only as good as your ability to truly comprehend and strategize with it.

I'll give you an example: At the end of each year, Spotify provides artists with a yearly roundup of their performance on the platform (you may have seen artists post these on social media). This is known as 'Spotify Wrapped' and typically includes things like the total number of streams, listeners, and listening hours accrued over the past 12 months — as well as how many countries those streams came from.

Other platforms such as Apple Music and YouTube have also followed suit. For most artists, the typical assumption is likely 'the more streams, the better' — which is partially true, but not totally reflective of one's overall success on Spotify or any other digital service provider.

For example, an artist with 370,000 streams and 160,000 listeners averages out at about 2-3 streams per listener. However an artist with say 170,000 streams and 30,000 listeners averages at about 5-6 streams per listener (unless they are intentionally inflating their numbers). Meaning, an artist with fewer streams and fewer monthly listeners may be doing a better job at retaining and growing their audience over one with what appears to have "bigger" and "better" numbers. Reasons for this could be the artist with more overall streams using methods like:

Playlist-driven traffic: Benefiting from algorithmic or editorial playlist placements that drive one-time listens without a strategy to convert them to loyal fans.

Viral trends: They may have had a song go viral on social media, leading to a surge in casual listeners who don't engage further with their catalog.

Poorly-targeted ads: Heavy investment in paid ads or sponsored content targeting listeners outside their core audience while not paying attention to conversion rates. They could also be failing to assess the initial/organic performance of their content to ensure they are ramping up promotional efforts on the content their followers have been most responsive to. (Sometimes, what you think is your best material versus what your audience gleans more towards are not aligned. Data helps to close that gap.)

Broad but shallow appeal: Their music might have mass appeal but lack the depth to encourage repeat listens or exploration of their wider catalog.

Poor fan engagement: They may not be effectively engaging with their audience, missing opportunities to build real connections.

Inconsistent quality: Their catalog might be inconsistent, with one or two popular tracks but additional content with lesser quality.

Lack of brand identity: Lacking a strong artist brand that resonates with listeners and encourages further exploration of their material.

Clickbait Marketing: Misleading acquisition tactics to drive traffic — e.g. using titles, thumbnails, or other lead magnets that do not necessarily relate to the content.

In most of these cases, there is a strong possibility the artist is not focusing their efforts in the right areas and, as a result, may achieve a poor retention rate — leaving them with "high" streaming numbers without much authentic community growth and/or engagement.

Another key data factor that can impact your artist reach and growth on platforms such as Spotify is how your collaborations are credited. If a featured artist is listed as a 'co-main' or 'co-primary' artist instead of a 'featured artist', Spotify's algorithms will treat the track as a joint release by *both* artists (and not one 'featuring' the other).

This means the song will have the same level of visibility on both artists' profiles, and be equally pushed to both of their audiences, with each listener of the track added to both artists' monthly listener counts — boosting both of their reaches. However, if the collaborator is only credited as a 'featured artist', Spotify will treat the release differently, limiting how much of the featured artist's audience it pushes the song to.

For instance, when WaterTower Music and Interscope Records enlisted Atlanta rapper Lil Baby and gospel artist Kirk Franklin for the song "We Win" on the Space Jam 2 soundtrack, Franklin was credited as a 'co-main artist'. Given this, the song appears in the *main* discography section of both artists' profiles, equally exposing and recommending the track to both of their audiences.

Had Franklin been listed as a featured artist, the song would still appear on his profile, but only in the "Appears On" section at the very bottom (resulting in less visibility), which would be a missed opportunity for Lil Baby to capture and convert a larger portion of Franklin's fan base.

Understanding these factors and metrics is becoming increasingly important for artists to be able to ensure they are effectively sustaining and growing their community, rather than just 'chasing numbers' to impress others or for self-gratification. This is an opportune moment to delve into one of the most discussed and perplexing subtopics related specifically to data, reach, and growth on any digital platform: algorithms.

At its most basic level, an algorithm is a piece of digital data (information) in the form of a set of step-by-step instructions designed to perform a particular task. When it comes to user-driven digital media platforms (Instagram, Spotify, TikTok, YouTube, etc), these algorithms typically have two main goals: to keep you on the platform for as long as possible and encourage you to return.

Just as these digital media platforms strive to maximize user engagement and retention, artists should also prioritize the same. The more time users spend interacting with and returning to your content, the more you can build stronger fan relationships and cultivate a thriving community.

Though algorithms are often referred to as singular (e.g. statements like "the algorithm has changed"), most digital platforms with large user bases like say Instagram, Netflix, and Spotify for example, typically have up to hundreds of different algorithms in order to function the way they do.

For instance, one of the Spotify algorithms analyzes consumer listening history (including how much of a song you listen to before skipping — which we touched on earlier), as well as liked/saved songs, and pretty much any and all of your interactions to understand your preferences. It then uses this data to create personalized playlists like 'Discover Weekly', 'Release Radar', 'Daily Drive', and 'Daylist' that suggest new songs and artists you might like based on your (and similar users') tastes. Much of these processes are also reliant on metadata (we'll get that into in a moment).

Another good example of a Spotify algorithm is the 'Radio' algorithm. This one creates personalized radio stations based on a particular song or artist, similar to Pandora's format [37]. It considers characteristics such as genre, mood, tempo, and different forms of metadata to curate a playlist of music similar to the chosen song or artist.

Just like the previous example above, this algorithm also takes into account the user's listening history and preferences to deliver a 'radio station' that aligns with their musical taste, allowing for another type of tailored listening experience. Consequently, two users starting a Billie Eilish radio station might experience significantly different playlists, each tailored to their individual listening habits and preferences relevant to Eilish's music.

Despite this becoming somewhat of a trend across the board, trying to understand and take advantage of all of the different algorithms and their specific rules will have you chasing your tail forever. Many of them undergo frequent changes and most platforms do not publicly disclose precise details on how they work. However, through research clues and A/B testing, some of the more foundational algorithms are occasionally uncovered.

These "staple algorithms" form the fundamental framework that shapes how platforms operate and, whilst they may evolve, will rarely undergo drastic changes that steer from the platform's main goal of keeping you engaged for as long as they can [38]. For this reason, these "staple algorithms" are the only ones that might be worth actually "chasing" — just like the Spotify ones laid out above. In terms of how to take advantage of these 'staple' algorithms, here are a few ways you can do so:

Optimize for the 'Radio' algorithm:

- Create playlists featuring your music alongside similar artists in your genre.
- Collaborate with artists who have a similar sound to increase your chances of appearing in their artist radio station playlist.

Leverage the 'Discover Weekly' and similar personalized playlists:

- Encourage your existing fans to save your songs to their playlists and libraries, as this increases the likelihood of your music being recommended to similar listeners.
- Consistently release new music to stay relevant in these algorithmic playlists.

Focus on retention rates:

- Use seamless transitions between tracks to encourage continuous play (Beyoncé's 'Renaissance' album is a great reference for this).
- Place your strongest, most engaging tracks early in your album, EP, or playlist tracklist to hook listeners early, encouraging them to continue through the entire collection

(reducing the likelihood of early skips).

Engage with platform-specific features:

- Create and share Spotify Canvas videos for your tracks, as well as 'Clips'.
- Use the lyrics feature to add time-synced lyrics to your songs. Doing so gives listeners another engagement touchpoint while listening to your music.

Encourage user-generated content:

- Run campaigns that encourage fans to create content using your music, which can increase engagement and potentially trigger algorithmic boosts.

In addition to the above, another key part of how these 'staple' algorithms execute themselves on digital music streaming services is based on metadata; an often overlooked but *extremely* important element of music administration.

Metadata includes information like song titles, genre classifications, release dates, composers, artist information, and more. This data provides the foundation for algorithms to understand and categorize music and plays a significant role in creating personalized recommendations, generating playlists, and enhancing the overall user experience. Think of metadata as part of your music's search engine optimization (SEO) strategy on streaming services.

Just like a well-optimized website uses specific keywords and information to rank highly in relevant search results, your music's metadata helps it surface in the right playlists, recommendations, and search queries, ultimately connecting your songs with the most prime and receptive listeners. The more accurate and detailed information you provide within your track files and/or to your digital distributor, the easier it becomes to discover and curate your music to a wider and appropriate audience.

Some of the aspects of metadata that artists often do not consider are things like comprehensive genre tags (with subgenres), mood, descriptors, and other lesser-known tags like campaign affiliations (which we'll get into later). Though, understanding the importance of these tags is just the beginning. Ensuring you choose *relevant* and *specific* tags that accurately represent the style and sound of the music is even more critical.

Let's go back to subgenres for a moment: avoiding sticking with broad or generic genres can help ensure that the music is appropriately categorized and recommended to the right listeners.

For instance, instead of only listing "Hip Hop" as a track genre, you can add "Mumble Rap" as a subgenre (if applicable) to reach a more specific audience. What's the difference, you ask, and will it *actually* help?! Well, a hardcore fan of iconic traditional hip hop group Wu-Tang Clan may not necessarily appreciate a recommendation of Atlanta 'mumble' rapper Young Thug's latest single to the same degree that a hardcore fan of mumble rap group Migos might, even though all three artists fall under the "Hip Hop" genre.

A more interesting type of metadata is using tags to include the name of a brand, campaign, TV show, or movie a song may be associated with. To illustrate, if you were to type in "White Chicks" on Spotify, one of (if not) the first songs to pop up is "A Thousand Miles" by Vanessa Carlton — due to the fact that many associate the song with its inclusion in the 'White Chicks' movie. Interestingly, the song was already out prior to the movie, and the studio behind "White Chicks" never officially released a movie soundtrack compilation.

This suggests that, to take advantage of its new popular association with the film, the movie title may have been tagged in the metadata for the song on digital service providers after "White Chicks" was released. Additionally, playlists created by fans may have played a role in Spotify's algorithm understanding the song's connection to the film. This is yet another one of the benefits of music in the digital landscape; metadata can be constantly updated to reflect new associations and connections between songs and various media so your music reaches the right audience.

As the music industry continues its evolution, the value of all types of data and the importance of data analysis will progressively heighten. For years now, labels and other music companies have collectively spent huge amounts of capital every year to access extremely high-level data platforms like Luminate (formerly Nielsen SoundScan, which lists record sales data) — and there's a reason why. Without it, it is difficult to understand the current climate of the market, thereby making it difficult to gain a sense of direction and gauge success in the right context.

Just as an example of how much major companies value data insights, Spotify spent $66 million to acquire music intelligence company The Echo Nest in 2014 to help them learn more about user behavior and perfect their algorithms [39]. The following year, Apple purchased British start-up and music analytics company Semetric for a deal valued at $50 million by the Financial Times [40].

Data does not only reflect where you as an artist may need

to focus more of your efforts (such as understanding where and what merchandise to sell or deciding which of your songs should have a music video — e.g. Chris Brown's decision to release a video for the 2019-released song "Under the Influence" in 2022, after it saw a 'late' surge in popularity on TikTok). More significantly, data allows you to evaluate and communicate your worth — which is determined by the strength of your community. Armed with this information, you can better grasp your bargaining power and ensure that the opportunities you seek align with your current career status.

Using a hypothetical situation, pitching to perform on a Coachella stage with say 50,000 stagnant or fluctuating monthly listeners on Spotify will probably not yield the desired result... (at least not yet). However, 500,000 steadily *growing* monthly listeners is likely to attract a booking agent that they work with at the very least — thereby increasing your chances of landing a slot at some point.

Even beyond informing your bargaining power and helping you align opportunities, data can also provide valuable insights into your potential for success in international markets. A deep analysis of your streaming and social media metrics may lead you to discover that your music resonates strongly with audiences in regions far from your 'home base' or where you've been focusing your marketing.

To demonstrate, a singer-songwriter based in Europe might find that their biggest fan base is somewhere in South America, or a rapper from the United States may have a surprisingly large following in an Asian region. Insights like this can help you prioritize your international outreach efforts and tailor your strategy in order to capitalize on your global appeal.

If you notice that your music is gaining significant traction in a region like say Japan, but your lyrics are primarily in English, it could be worth partnering with a Japanese lyricist or translator to create a version of your most popular songs with Japanese lyrics to optimize your appeal to that market and demonstrate your commitment to engaging with your audience on a more meaningful level.

Alternatively, you could consider collaborating with another artist who is also popular in that region (even if they are not physically based there) — something that can be discovered by monitoring local or regional charts and playlists.

The beauty of our interconnected digital age is that geographical boundaries no longer limit creative partnerships; two artists gaining traction in the same market can easily collaborate on a track, exchanging ideas and files online, without ever needing to be in the same room or even meet in person. This, however, does not diminish the value of in-person connection in the creative process, which often gives more space to create a unique energy and spontaneity.

Strategic moves such as these can help you tap into a larger portion of a region where you are already gaining momentum and create music that resonates more deeply within the cultural context of that particular market.

With the ability to connect in more and more ways, the music industry will only continue to globalize, making these kinds of tactical partnerships even more crucial for sustainability and expansion. Recent rapid growth in regions like Asia, Latin America, and Sub-Saharan Africa (the fastest-growing continental region of 2023) has opened up more doors for growth, and artists who can effectively leverage data to understand and connect with diverse demographics will be best positioned to seize the most advantageous opportunities [41].

Several major international acts have used these types of approaches in the past. Aforementioned artists like Michael Jackson, for instance, recorded his 1987 song 'I Just Can't Stop Loving You' in both French and Spanish, due to the data (likely such as radio play, ticket sales, and chart positions) reflecting those to be two of his largest non-English markets at the time.

A more current example of this (proving such strategies to be timeless), is Big Hit Entertainment's K-pop supergroup, BTS. Initially, the group specifically prioritized singing in Korean (with occasional English phrases) — and saw groundbreaking success doing so.

In 2019, BTS member RM, the group's only fluent English speaker at the time, said the following in an interview with Entertainment Weekly: *"I don't want to compare, but I think it's even harder as an Asian group. A Hot 100 and a Grammy nomination, these are our goals. But they're just goals — we don't want to change our identity or our genuineness to get the No. 1."* (referring to the group's decision to sing exclusively in Korean) [42].

However, the COVID-19 pandemic led to a significant shift in BTS' strategy. In 2020, the group released 'Dynamite', their first fully English-language song. The song became their first #1 hit on the Billboard Hot 100. They followed up 'Dynamite' with two more English singles, "Butter" and "Permission to Dance," both of which also topped the coveted chart [43].

This pivot did not come without its challenges. One of the group's members, Jin, shared with Billboard that 'the English he learned in school was significantly different from the English in the song'. Nonetheless, with their 2020 world tour getting canceled due to the pandemic, BTS saw this as a necessary strategy to maintain their global momentum and reach new audiences. The success of these English-language tracks illustrates the importance of data-driven decision-making, even when it pushes you beyond your comfort zone.

Even though the pandemic-induced tour cancellation may have been the catalyst for BTS' English-language releases, data analysis would have likely played a crucial role in shaping this strategy. A few ways BTS and their team could have used data to inform this decision that independent artists can learn from are:

Market Resilience Analysis: Data research on how different markets were responding to the pandemic in terms of music consumption could have highlighted the need to focus on certain regions or languages.

Competitor Analysis: Data on how other global artists were maintaining their presence during lockdowns could have informed their strategy.

Fan Sentiment Analysis: They may have used AI-powered tools and services to analyze fan comments and posts, gauging the disappointment for the tour cancellation and appetite for new content from English-speaking global regions.

Another prime, but slightly different, example of leveraging data for international engagement is Beyoncé's embrace of diverse foreign cultures. In 2019, the Houston-born entertainer released the soundtrack album "The Lion King: The Gift". The project, which serves as a companion to both the "The Lion King" live-action remake (2019) and her Disney+ musical film "Black Is King", features an array of African artists, including

Wizkid, Shatta Wale, and Grammy Award Winner Burna Boy. Sonically, the LP incorporates elements of various African musical styles, such as Afrobeats and 'gqom' music (originating in South Africa).

Through her collaborations with these influential African figures from regions hugely growing in popularity, and paying homage to the continent's rich heritage, Beyoncé not only showcased her deep appreciation for African music and culture, but also introduced some of her global fan base to the vibrant and diverse music scenes that were already thriving across Africa (not unlike the impact of her 2024 release "Cowboy Carter" which shed light on black country acts like, but not limited to, Shaboozey, Linda Martell, and Brittney Spencer).

A more specific data-driven example is the 'Halo' star's collaborations in the Latin music world. In 2007, just a few months after the release of her 'Beautiful Liar' duet with Shakira, which performed exceptionally well in Latin markets (likely boosted in part by Shakira's presence on the track) Beyoncé went on to release a full Latin EP titled 'Irreemplazable' ('Irreplaceable' in Spanish). The project included Spanish versions of some of her biggest hits to date (at the time), such as 'Listen,' 'Irreplaceable,' and 'Beautiful Liar,' and featured collaborations with numerous prominent Latin artists.

This ploy catered to a significant portion of Beyoncé's Latin fan base, also enhancing her marketability and fan loyalty in a market where she had seen a recent surge in popularity as a result of collaborating with Shakira (a very well-calculated move).

Beyoncé's very intentional engagement with the Latin market did not end there. In 2017, she contributed to the remix of 'Mi Gente' by J Balvin and Willy William. The track was already popular in Spanish-speaking countries (and other parts of the world), however, the 30+ GRAMMY Award-winner's participation helped bridge her mainstream audience with J Balvin's reggaeton fan base. The remix became a cultural crossover hit, landing the #1 spot on Billboard's Hot Latin Songs Chart and receiving the Latin Rhythm Song of the Year Award at the 2018 Billboard Latin Music Awards [44].

As we can see, the success of these maneuvers (including the examples of Michael Jackson, BTS, and Beyoncé), which span numerous musical eras and centuries are all underpinned by data — and go beyond just random collaborations between your favorite artists. Under the surface, the specificity of these collaborative choices is reflective of comprehensive engagement strategies and deep dives into international cultures, informed by market analyses and an understanding of fan behavior across regions.

The most exciting part of this is that much of the same data used to make these decisions is widely available to independent artists today. Just as these megastars utilized data to bridge cultural gaps and cater to diverse audiences, independent artists can use similar strategies to enhance their global reach and connect more effectively with fans worldwide.

Remember, to build long-term success as opposed to exclusively experiencing random moments of success, it's crucial to use data not only to identify and celebrate your wins but to carefully analyze them as well.

Understanding what led to each success can inform future strategies and ensure sustained progress in your career over time. For example, let's say a fictional independent hip-hop artist named 'Benny Brim' puts out a new single that performs relatively well and hits 250,000 streams on Spotify in its first month (up from say his usual average of 50,000 streams per month, per track). Rather than simply basking in the glory of his victory, Benny takes a deep dive into the data behind this success by analyzing the following factors:

Timing: He dropped the single on a Friday, coinciding with Spotify's New Music Friday and Release Radar playlist update schedule.

Collaboration: The track features a popular artist from a different genre in a foreign region that both they and Benny are gaining momentum in, potentially expanding his audience.

Lyrical Content: The song addresses a current social issue, resonating strongly with old and new listeners.

Data: Benny notices a significant increase in listeners from a foreign region where he and his collaborator are popular.

Playlisting: As a result of the above, the track was picked up by various popular hip-hop and cross-genre editorial, algorithmic and user-generated playlists.

Variations: Benny releases numerous remixes of the song, including an acoustic version, a sped-up/slowed-down version (for TikTok), and a remix featuring another artist with similar or more popularity than himself. On that note, here's a fun fact: According to inside data from Luminate, almost 50% of the top 100 songs in the U.S. in 2024 had five different versions/variations.

Based on this analysis, Benny can inform her future strategies by:

- Timing future releases for Fridays to align with popular playlist updates.
- Pursuing more key collaborations to expand his audience.
- Consider addressing more current and timeless issues in his lyrics.
- Plan a tour or targeted marketing in the neighboring region to capitalize on the new audience there.
- Nurture relationships with playlist curators who supported this release.
- Ensure all future releases have numerous versions to increase the reach.

With all that said, it's essential to recognize that data strategies alone are not sufficient for building authentic connections with communities across different cultures. Truly succeeding in the global music market also requires a cultivation and understanding of the local nuances and sensibilities that make each region unique. Not just in terms of language and culture, but also considering things like the social and political contexts of the regions you are focusing on. In balancing data-driven analyses with a genuine appreciation for local cultures, you can execute strategies that truly create meaningful connections on a global scale.

The nuanced application of these data insights parallels the preparation required to perform on those prestigious platforms like Coachella, as we mentioned earlier. But while a Coachella aspiration might be a long shot for the average independent artist, the strategic use of data can help independent artists set and achieve more immediate, measurable goals that build towards larger career milestones that give you a concrete way to transform your data into opportunities.

Platforms like Spotify for Artists, Apple Music for Artists, YouTube Analytics, and general data from digital music distributors are among the available services that offer extremely valuable data insights for free.

There are also affordable offerings like SoundCharts, ChartMetric, and SongStats that afford anyone the chance to access even more intricate metrics on the market at large, providing perspective of the current landscape and your position within it. With these kinds of tools, you can easily perform tasks like comparative data analyses against your peers and/or your 'competition;', without having to break the bank or be a data expert.

Once you have a firm grasp of your data and have created a strategy around it (including key performance indicators), you are now in a better and more empowered position to approach conversations about contracts, partnerships, and offers that can significantly elevate your career — which brings us to our next chapter: Deals and The Law.

CHAPTER 4:
Navigating Deals & The Law

Disclaimer: I am not, nor have I ever been, a music lawyer or legal professional of any kind. Thus, nothing in this chapter should be deemed as 'legal advice' — but rather an 'industry professional' perspective based on my years of experience. If you are seeking legal advice, please contact a licensed attorney in your region who specializes in either music, entertainment, or IP/copyright law.

Deals and the law are vital components of the music industry and have a long (and somewhat complicated) history. Some of the oldest music laws were established in the late 18th century. In 1710, the UK government enacted the Statute of Anne (better known as The Copyright Act 1710) [45].

The Statute of Anne was the first law to grant music creators exclusive rights over their works. It was not until 80 years later, in 1790, that the first U.S. copyright law was enacted under the new United States Constitution [46]. This copyright legislation was directly modeled after the UK's 'Statute of Anne' and only protected those who owned copyrights to compositions (which are usually music composers and/or publishers), not sound recordings (usually owned by artists and/or record labels).

Although musical compositions were not specifically mentioned in the first U.S. copyright act and were not explicitly covered by U.S. copyright law until the amended U.S. Copyright Act of 1831, musical compositions (not recordings) were still protected under the original 1790 Act, but were categorized as 'books' (as they focused on musical authorship and not performance). [47]

It was not until 1972, almost 200 years after the first U.S. copyright act, that *recorded* music copyright laws were first introduced in the United States, though they were not the first nation to do so [48]. European countries such as Germany and the UK enacted these laws much earlier (1901 and 1911, respectively [49][50]). The primary reason for these amendments was to extend copyright protection to sound recordings, which was relatively new technology at the time and had quickly become a largely profitable business, paving the way for the music industry as we know it today.

To briefly explain how recorded music (sound recordings) differ from a musical composition: think of a composition as the architectural design for a building, while a sound recording is an actual construction of that building. The design itself can be constructed multiple times as "different" individual buildings (i.e. different sound recordings) by different construction workers (i.e. recording artists) and owned by different companies (i.e. labels), but the architectural designer/s (songwriters) and those who own the rights to the design (i.e. publishing companies) remain the exact same. The implementation of these copyright laws allowed for music deals, contracts, and transactions to not only be properly executed, but legally enforced.

According to multiple sources, including Sony Music's AWAL website and The Washington Post, the first-ever exclusive record deal was made between Eldridge R. Johnson's Victor

Talking Machine Company (which later evolved into Sony Music's RCA Records) and the Metropolitan Opera singer, Enrico Caruso [51] [52]. The lucrative terms of the deal, signed in 1904, stated that Caruso would record ten arias (a vocal solo opera song) for the Victor Talking Machine Company, for a payment of $4,000 per song (worth about $1.4 million total in 2024).

In addition, Caruso was to receive between 26-40% of royalties from sales of the recordings. This percentage amounted to about 40 cents per sale (or $14 in 2024 dollars) which was a groundbreaking deal at the time — and would even be today (especially for a new artist with no data demonstrating their profitability).

In stark contrast to Caruso's deal, modern record deals for new artists typically offer much less favorable terms. Today, a typical new artist might receive an advance in the low-to-mid five figures, expected to cover recording costs and living expenses for a period of time (not to mention potential manager and attorney fees).

Royalty rates for new artists often range from 12-18% of *net* revenue [53] (the 'net' part is *very* important to note). This is, of course, significantly lower than Caruso's 26-40%. Moreover, unlike Caruso's straightforward deal, modern contracts often include clauses for multiple revenue streams beyond recorded music, such as merchandising and touring income (commonly known as a 360 deal). While the potential for success remains, the financial reward has largely shifted further toward the label in many cases, making Caruso's century-old deal seem remarkably artist-friendly by today's standards.

Due to his success, Caruso received a renewed deal from Victor in 1919, guaranteeing him $100,000 per year (worth

$1.8 million in 2024), *plus* royalties. At the time, a typical performer's salary was $15,000 (worth $280,000 in 2024). In comparison, ZipRecruiter and Salary.com estimate that the average U.S. artist's salary in 2024 is around $60,000. It is certainly worth noting that deals like Caruso's (and others at the time) were being offered in a *much* less saturated music industry with minimal pathways to success. With that came some cons, but it also brought significant benefits to the artists that did land deals or major opportunities, as they were facing much less competition in the marketplace — a benefit for both them and the record labels.

Despite the favorable terms of Caruso's deal, the landscape for artists shifted significantly in the ensuing decades. As the recording industry grew in the early to mid-20th century, record labels gained more power and leverage in negotiations. The Great Depression of the 1930s further affected deal terms, as companies sought to minimize financial risks. Then, following World War II, the explosion of popular music in the 1950s and 1960s led to increased competition among artists, which in turn gave labels greater bargaining power [54].

This period coincided with the famous "British Invasion" (when an array of British rock-and-roll groups became hugely popular in the U.S.) [55]. It was also the time we saw the rise of corporate consolidation, with larger companies acquiring smaller labels and 'standardizing' deal structures (often making them less favorable for artists).

Additionally, advancements in recording technology increased production costs, prompting labels to include terms in their contracts to offset these expenses. By the 1970s, market saturation allowed labels to offer less favorable terms to new, unproven talent who would later become icons, such as Prince (which we covered in the first chapter). The culmination of these industry shifts set the stage for further complications down the line.

As technology rapidly evolved, the rise of the digital music era brought about new challenges for music law, affecting deals and creating numerous "gray areas". The introduction of new revenue models (such as streaming services, user-generated content (UGC) monetization, 360 deals, and more) added another layer of complexity to deal negotiations.

Determining how these "new" revenue models would affect areas like artist compensation and revenue distribution is still very much a contentious topic, requiring industry players to navigate uncharted legal waters. Consequently, laws have had to continuously adapt to ensure both artists and entities remain protected for the use of their work.

One of these laws is the Digital Millennium Copyright Act (DMCA) introduced in 1998 [56]. The DMCA was enacted in response to the challenges posed by the digital age and the ease with which copyrighted materials could be distributed, shared, and copied online — something that the music industry never had to worry about previously.

The relatively new law, which creators and lawmakers have since proposed to update [57], includes provisions that limit the liability of internet service providers (like YouTube and Facebook) for infringing material posted by users, as long as they follow certain procedures for responding to infringement claims. This is why you may see copyright claims pop up on content you post to social media channels that feature popular music or visuals.

Amidst changing laws and the impact of the digital age on the music industry, the type of deals being offered to emerging artists have also undergone numerous changes. These shifts ultimately took the financial burden of artist development away from labels and investors, and put the onus of development on the artists themselves — with many labels, for the most part, now expecting talent to essentially be 'finished products' from the onset.

Now, with the ability to access vital data (like streaming numbers, social media engagement, live show demand, and other key metrics), labels can make more informed decisions about which artists to sign and, more importantly, how to structure their deal offerings. While this meant that traditional artist development would become a "thing of the past", there is a critical silver lining here for independent creators.

During the earlier days of the industry when labels signed artists purely based on talent with no track record of sales (particularly from the 1930s onward), even with good legal representation, many of them were unable to secure deals that leaned in their favor in the early stages of their careers, simply because they lacked the necessary bargaining power.

Where there is no verifiable data, there is no proof of concept — and without proof of concept, there is no surefire way to determine or communicate your value in the marketplace. These days, however, artists can take the time to build their worth, coming to the table more prepared to go into business with labels as a 'partner' and not a 'product' (which should be your goal for *any* deal). Atlanta rapper Russ is a great example of this.

Before signing with Columbia Records in 2017, Russ had been releasing a new song every week to his Soundcloud account, building his community [58]. This was after he'd already released a total of 11 albums and 87 singles independently that did not achieve any notable success but still allowed him to develop a loyal following.

As a result of these consistent independent releases, two of the songs Russ released on Soundcloud ("What They Want" and "Losin Control") ended up becoming Billboard Hot 100 hits in 2017. This led to him entering a 'partnership' agreement with Sony Music's Columbia Records. Under this partnership deal, Columbia would cover costs for the marketing and distribution of Russ' next three albums (until he left Columbia in 2020 and reverted to full independence).

In a 'partnership' deal (also known as a profit split agreement), artists and labels (depending on the deal) may equally share ownership of the master recordings (as opposed to a traditional record deal where labels will retain full ownership of the masters) — and profits are split *equally*, not in favor of either party.

The benefit of this for artists is that they often start seeing royalties a lot sooner and at a much higher rate. In a traditional deal, the artist's share of profits is significantly lower than the label's. Also, the artist is much more likely to spend a lot more time repaying their advance through a system that heavily favors the label's financial interests than they will be receiving any profits (more on this in the next chapter).

By the time he signed with Columbia, Russ had already released 300 songs and was touring extensively as an independent act. With this, he came to the table with significant value, giving him the leverage needed to sign a favorable deal.

Similar to Russ' former 50/50 'partnership deal' with Columbia, licensing agreements and other types of record deals have also emerged as the music industry evolved, as will more types of recording agreements over time — and creators, both independent and major, need to prepare for them.

For example, the idea of "smart" contracts (via blockchain technology) becoming standard practice in the music industry has been a topic of conversation amongst creators and professionals over recent years [59] [60]. Matter of fact, several music companies have already made it a part of their technology.

In 2018, Audius, a decentralized music streaming platform, emerged as a Web3 innovation, shifting the traditional artist-fan dynamic [61]. Supported by investors like Nas, Katy Perry, and Steve Aoki, and used by artists such as deadmau5, Skrillex, and Diplo, Audius was the first music streaming service to partner with TikTok and offer a unique model where artists freely host and distribute their music, earning direct revenue with no 'middleman' [62]. Unlike conventional subscription-based services, Audius operates without user fees, allowing anyone to publish and listen to music.

Central to Audius is its native cryptocurrency, $AUDIO, which is used to compensate artists for streams and offers staking rewards. The platform's decentralized structure, with music distributed across a global network of nodes (more on this shortly), potentially provides a more open and censorship-resistant system. It also introduces an alternative approach to artist remuneration through its use of cryptocurrency and smart contracts, while implementing a governance protocol that allows both artists and listeners to participate in platform decisions, exemplifying the ethos of Web3 in the music industry.

Of course, Audius is just one player in the evolving landscape and is yet to become a major force in the business, but its model highlights several ways new technology (such as blockchain) could possibly influence the music industry:

1. Increased transparency in royalty payments.
2. More direct artist-fan interactions and support mechanisms.
3. Decentralized platform governance.
4. New forms of music ownership and engagement through tokenization.

If adopted more widely, these innovations could significantly alter the industry's power dynamics, potentially giving artists and fans more control over music distribution and monetization (which has been an unspoken industry pattern for decades).

However, it's important to note that Audius and similar platforms are still in their early stages, and their long-term impact on the broader music industry remains to be seen. The value and success of a cryptocurrency like $AUDIO, or any platform-specific token, depends on several key factors. These include the currency's practical uses, its popularity, its availability and distribution, the platform's growth and improvements, overall market interest, and the legal landscape surrounding cryptocurrencies.

Despite all the media conversations surrounding new technologies and processes like the ones mentioned above, there is still a lot of clarity that can be provided as to how exactly they work, and more specifically, how they can impact the music industry and help independent artists.

Let's take blockchain. Although it only started to become a hot topic during the 2010s due to the rise of Bitcoin, the concept of blockchains is over thirty years old.

In 1991, cryptographers Stuart Haber and Scott Stornetta introduced a cryptographically secure chain of blocks containing timestamped data, which was designed to prevent the backdating of digital documents [63]. While their initial use cases were focused on securing digital documents, their work laid the foundation for the development of blockchain technology today.

Currently, in order for artists to receive compensation from the deals they secure, they have to rely on honest accounting from record companies, publishers, distributors, digital music service providers, and, sometimes, even concert promotion companies. Beyond that, their payments may have to go through additional parties before reaching them, whether that be managers, accountants, booking agents, etc. One of the issues this has created, even in the best of cases, is there can sometimes be discrepancies, under-reporting, and general accounting errors. This is usually addressed by auditing.

During a 2014 interview with Canada's BNN Bloomberg to promote his fifth studio and first independent album 'Animal Ambition', Curtis '50 Cent' Jackson spoke about his exit from Interscope Records [64]. He mentioned that when the time came for him to leave the label, they conducted an audit to ensure there were not any outstanding payments due. After a nine-year audit had been completed by Interscope, Jackson stated that the label ended up owing him a total of $23 million in unpaid royalties. Now, one may ask "How do you *not* know you owe an artist an amount of the magnitude?". But, it happens, and often. And the challenge is that the average signed artist cannot afford the costs that come with an audit.

Due to the complexity of the work involved, not only does an audit require what can be costly legal representation and labor, but a lot of artists fear that requesting one could affect their relationship with their label or publisher — which could be why 50 Cent waited until the end of his deal with Interscope before requesting one. The music industry employing blockchain technology and smart contracts could completely eradicate this long-standing problem, creating a much more transparent and streamlined process.

We have heard a lot about it, but what exactly is a blockchain? A blockchain is a decentralized database that maintains a constantly growing list of digital transactions and asset ownership, stored in digitally connected 'blocks' (or 'ledgers' which you could refer to as a group of receipts) — hence the term 'blockchain'. These 'blocks' each contain unique information and are distributed on a wide network of computers (also referred to as 'nodes') [63].

Because the transactions are distributed to such a large network that anyone with a computer and internet connection can become a part of with no central authority, it is resistant to almost any type of hack, making it extremely difficult to successfully manipulate its data [65].

To illustrate, imagine you want to send money to a friend of yours. Your friend provides you with a 'digital key' of some sort (similar to a checking account/routing number), and you then type up all that information into a Google document, including how much money you are sending.

This document represents the transaction details on the blockchain (ledger). After you have entered all that information the Google document is shared with thousands or millions of others (i.e. added to the blockchain), signifying the completion and verification of the transaction. However, after it has been completed, let's say the document's editing access is now locked and it is now permanently a 'read-only' file (hiding any 'sensitive' data), even for the person who created it. That is essentially how blockchain transactions work.

The key difference between blockchains versus a Google document is that if any individual tries to hack and/or edit the final read-only document, the blockchain will identify who (which computer/node) attempted to make the change. The system will then reject it and permanently cut off that computer's access to the network. Thus, instead of relying on a central authority like a bank to verify the transaction, it relies on the data being consistent across the entire network — and, if at any point it becomes inconsistent, it automatically corrects itself and blocks the source where the change came from.

Another way to look at it is by imagining a game of 'Chinese whispers' in which everyone has to whisper the exact same message into their neighbor's ear, but instead, everyone is speaking out loud — and anyone that 'breaks the chain' by changing the message is removed from the game, allowing it to continue with one consistent message.

Blockchains also go beyond just keeping note of digital transactions. They can also include ownership details of unique digital assets (such as the once-very-popular NFTs), which is where it can really come in handy in the music industry — particularly with the use of things like smart contracts.

Smart contracts are self-executing agreements between two parties that automatically trigger based on if-then logic (meaning if a condition is met, then an action is executed — not unlike an algorithm) [66]. You could technically call them AI contracts. These contracts are stored on a blockchain — thereby increasing financial transparency and payment frequency, and decreasing room for accounting errors. With smart contracts, artists could automatically be compensated (based on whatever payment schedule is set in the contract) anytime a rule is triggered.

For example, an independent artist releases a song on a music platform that uses blockchain technology. The platform or artist then sets up a smart contract that outlines the terms of payment for the song's streams that is programmed to automatically execute payments every time the song reaches say 50,000 streams. It could also have another trigger that executes monthly once the song starts achieving 100,000 streams per month, for example. These same clauses could also be included in a record label agreement, providing the label also integrates blockchain tech and smart contracts.

As stated by British recording artist Imogen Heap, who trialed smart contracts with her song "Tiny Human" in 2018, "creatives are often first to put in any work and the last to get paid" [67]. The smart contract method could change this by eliminating the need for lengthy reporting and payment cycles typically associated with traditional music distribution methods.

Through the blockchain's transparent ledger (or a similar type of technology yet to come), artists could easily monitor the progress of a song's streams and payments through the blockchain's ledger. Furthermore, since the smart contract is secure and 'tamper-proof', they can trust that the payments will be executed as defined in the contract — without having to worry about an audit.

Whether it be blockchain technology, smart contracts, or another future form of tech, these methods have the potential to revolutionize the way artists are compensated, but they're not the only emerging technologies that are well-positioned to shake up industry traditions. As we've discussed earlier, artificial intelligence (AI) is another major player that is rapidly making its mark.

In August 2023, YouTube partnered with Universal Music Group to launch their Music AI Incubator. As part of their statement announcing the initiative, they stated *Advancements in generative AI are no longer a future promise"* — insinuating that AI developments are not the future, they are the present [68]. Consequently, these advancements have already been affecting record deals and will likely force necessary updates to music-related laws, especially considering the capabilities of AI-generated music.

Given the potential impact of these technological advancements on the music industry, it cannot be denied that there is great importance in always being ready and prepared for what is next so you can position yourself accordingly. But if there is anything you need to understand about deals, it is this: Your leverage in *any* case will always rely on your data, and your data is a reflection of the strength of your community. Additionally, as with most deals in the music industry, the ultimate goal is typically an increased profile and/or financial gain — which is where the importance of capital comes in, as the fifth and final staple.

CHAPTER 5:
The Flow of Capital

From the inception of the music industry, capital has been an integral component. Labels, musicians, and other involved entities have always needed some form of funding to record, produce, market, perform, and distribute their music.

Even at the very basic level, aside from the production and promotion of music, capital is essential for personal sustainability as a music creative and/or professional — just like in any other industry/career. However, the necessity of capital in the music industry extends well beyond the realm of personal sustainability for its creatives and professionals. Its economic reach also spills over to other sectors, impacting a range of businesses and service providers.

For instance, a music concert tour doesn't just generate revenue for the artists and production teams; it also boosts income for local businesses, from hospitality companies to transportation services and beyond. According to Forbes, Beyoncé's 2023 Renaissance World Tour contributed $4.5 billion to the U.S. economy — comparable to the economic impact of the 2008 Olympics on Beijing [69].

This domino effect of financial activity demonstrates the music industry's role as more than a cultural phenomenon, but also as a vital cog in the wheel of the broader economic system. Out of all of the funding streams provided by the music industry's ecosystem, one of the oldest and most substantial revenue sources stems from live performances — dating back centuries before the industry was 'officially' birthed.

Attested by Patricia Spencer in Volume 66 of the 'Near Eastern Archaeology' journal (No. 3), professional dancers and musicians would often be enlisted to perform in the Ancient Egyptian city of Bacchias (between the third century BC and fourth century AD) for payments of 36 drachmas per day (approximately $2,000 USD per day in 2024) [70] [71]. This was significantly higher than the average daily rate for labor in other industries at the time, which was less than 3 drachmas (approximately $175 in 2024), partly due to the inconsistent employment opportunities for entertainers — not unlike the reality for most modern-day creatives.

During more recent times, additional income streams began to arise, with the introduction of music publishing companies that would pay composers for the rights to publish their music (initially just as sheet music), and would then sell that sheet music to the public so others could read and perform it. One of the first publishing companies was Breitkopf & Härtel, launched in 1719 (though the origin of printed, reproducible sheet music dates back to 1476 with Roman printer Ulrich Han's Missale Romanum [72]). Breitkopf & Härtel still exists today as the world's oldest music publisher and is most famous for publishing J.S. Bach's sheet music.

Later on (as we discussed earlier) record labels came into the picture and became one of the primary sources of capital, particularly for recording artists. New talent would sign contracts with record labels, which provided them with the

CHAPTER 5: THE FLOW OF CAPITAL

funding needed to record and distribute their work, in exchange for ownership of their master recordings and a significant percentage of revenue from their releases. On the topic of signing record deals, it would probably not be a surprise if I were to advise artists to ensure they understand the intricacies of their deals before signing (as we went over in the previous chapter). But, with deals having such a huge direct connection to capital, I would be remiss not to continue with that topic somewhat in this chapter.

I would say most people probably know that when you sign a traditional record deal, whatever advance or budget a label gives you has to be recouped from your earnings before you start seeing any money. However, there is an element to this that many likely do not know: the money that you need to recoup is deducted exclusively from the artist's share of royalties, not the label's.

For example, with a good lawyer on your team, you may get a 17% royalty rate on a typical record deal. Now, let's say you are given a $500,000 album budget — the general perception is "once the label 'breaks even' on that $500,000, I'll start earning my share of royalties". While that may be the case for other types of investments, it is not the case for traditional record deals.

In reality, you will actually need to generate six times that amount ($3 million) for the label, before you start earning any royalties. To break it down further, the label would need to make $2.5 million in profit from your project, before you see a penny. That's about 750 million streams on Spotify. This should not be taken as advice against signing a traditional deal, but rather just a piece of critical information to ensure you are aware of what could be referred to as the 'devil in the detail'.

Although deal clauses like these still exist today, the types of record deals offered to artists have significantly evolved — and will continue to do so. With the current prominence of digital streaming services, brand partnerships, increased demand for touring and merchandise (particularly after the COVID-19 pandemic), and a new revolutionary wave of artificial intelligence on the horizon, label structures and offerings have had to not only evolve but adapt — creating more revenue streams and adjusting their business models to increase profitability for themselves and the artists they represent.

For example, some years back, Sony Music launched 'The Thread Shop'; a merchandise division that specializes in creating and selling merchandise for Sony's artists and other brands. The Thread Shop (now under the 'Ceremony of Roses' merchandise banner [73]) has since expanded to become a leading merchandising company in the music industry — producing, selling, and marketing official merch for artists such as DJ Khaled, The Beatles, Elvis Presley, Michael Jackson, Lil Nas X, 21 Savage, and more.

This is not a typical function of a record label, but one that many labels have embraced to diversify their income sources and remain afloat while offering artists an established and efficient platform to boost their merchandising businesses. Doing so can enhance the artists' brand reach and fan engagement without the complexities of handling production and distribution themselves.

In recent years, music financing companies (like Sound Royalties and beatBread) have also emerged as new sources of funding for artists. Similar to labels, these companies provide artists with advances in exchange for a percentage of their future earnings. The major difference here is that these financing companies do not require you to sign away the rights to your catalog — something typically mandatory in most record labels or licensing agreements. This model allows artists to maintain more control over their music and careers while still receiving the necessary funding to produce and distribute their work.

Moreover, the rise of blockchain technology and cryptocurrencies has introduced new possibilities for artists to raise capital and engage with their fans. Platforms like Audius (covered earlier) and Viberate are leveraging blockchain to create decentralized music ecosystems that empower artists with more control over their content and earnings [74]. On Audius, for example, artists can issue their own 'tokens' for purchase, allowing fans to directly invest in their careers and potentially even share in their success [75].

The specifics vary by platform, however, such technologies can potentially enable new forms of artist-fan interactions that allow fans to support and engage with artists' careers in more direct and innovative ways. This model not only provides a new funding avenue but also strengthens the artist-fan relationship.

These innovative funding models, including music financing companies and blockchain-based platforms, differ from traditional platforms like Spotify and even artist crowdfunding services, giving artists more financial autonomy.

So with the industry, so with artists attempting to break into the industry. As industry revenue streams have expanded, and will continue to expand, the key as an artist is ensuring you tap into these various new ways to acquire capital (while maximizing the traditional ways) to fund both your career and personal life.

Typical revenue sources (generated from record sales etc)

have dramatically declined for a lot of music creators and have almost become non-existent in some cases, with sustainable income from streaming requiring stats that are often unattainable for the average independent artist. Fortunately, there are still so many other ways capital can be generated. Here are just a few:

1. Branded merchandise (unique, high-quality merch with messaging that aligns with your brand).

2. Revenue from live shows (also including virtual, corporate, and private events).

3. Offering songwriting, music, and vocal production, mixing, or mastering services to other artists.

4. Selling music samples or loops through online platforms like Splice or Loopmasters.

5. Offering vocal coaching or instrument lessons.

6. Selling tickets to exclusive listening parties, virtual concerts, or meet-and-greets.

7. Writing and selling eBooks and/or courses on music production.

8. Participating in sync licensing opportunities for the use of your music in TV shows, films, video games, advertisements, and other media.

9. Crowdfunding for new projects, music videos, or album production.

10. Monetizing social media accounts through subscriptions, affiliate marketing, or sponsored posts.

11. Creating and licensing music for production libraries used in media.

12. Partnering with a software developer to develop and sell AI tools for music composition.

13. Brand deals and partnerships.

These alternative revenue streams offer immense evergreen earning potential, but it's crucial to approach them with a well-thought-out strategy. Each avenue requires meticulous planning, execution, and alignment with your unique brand and target audience.

Haphazardly pursuing multiple revenue sources without a clear strategy increases the chances of wasted efforts and ending up with subpar results. Just because the idea sounds exciting, it does not mean it is best for you to pursue right now. But by developing a well-defined plan that considers your strengths, resources, available marketplace tools, and fan base, you can effectively harness some of these tactics to generate a sustainable income.

One example of a successful artist who utilized some of the above tactics to raise capital to finance their career is Amanda Palmer — an independent artist and author known for her successful crowdfunding. In 2012, Palmer launched a

Kickstarter campaign to fund her second studio album "Theatre is Evil", as well as a supporting tour. Palmer set a goal of just $100,000 but ended up raising over $1.2 million from more than 24,000 backers from her community [76]. The campaign became one of the most successful music campaigns in Kickstarter history at the time.

Following the success of the campaign and the subsequent album (which reached the top 10 on the Billboard 200 chart [77]), Palmer released a book entitled "The Art of Asking," which chronicled her experiences with crowdfunding and the relationships between artists and their fans. The book landed her a spot on the NY Times bestsellers list and multiple speaking engagements — including TED talks. All of this stemmed from the strength of Amanda's community and her commitment to developing it.

Selling merchandise (whether it be books, shirts, or vinyl records), has been one of the most profitable alternative revenue streams for recording artists. For the average artist, if you are not selling merch you are likely missing out on an extra $10,000 USD per year (on average). This is per Spotify data [78]. However, many independent artists struggle to successfully sell merchandise because they don't understand their target audiences. Let's explore this further:

On leading streaming platforms like Spotify, you would need to generate an estimated 3,800 streams to gross $15 (according to streamingroyaltycalculator.com). Comparatively, you could potentially earn that same amount by selling just one t-shirt.

However, relying solely on t-shirt sales without considering your audience's preferences can limit your revenue potential. It is critically important to leverage data to understand what your fans are interested in purchasing, so you can offer a more diverse and appealing range of products that align with their desires to maximize your earnings.

Data from artist merchandise management company Merch Cat shows that 85% of artist merchandise is sold at live shows [79]. To properly take advantage of these moments, while your fans are present and emotionally engaged in the moment, it is essential to offer items that resonate most in the cities where you are performing. Even if touring minimally, streaming analytics can provide insight into where your fan base is geographically concentrated.

For instance, a Fan Study by Spotify revealed variances in merch preferences across regions. Music fans in London purchase more t-shirts and hoodies than any other city but buy much fewer hats and bags (Los Angeles ranks #1 for both). Further segmentation by genre indicates vinyl records and CDs sell exceptionally well among fans in Seattle and Phoenix (respectively). Vinyl also sells very well amongst R&B, Hip Hop, and EDM fans [80].

Optimizing profitability as an artist requires diverse product offerings that cater to different fan segments and their varying levels of commitment to your music, especially with the industry's growing focus on 'superfans' (as we went over in the first chapter). This may include items at various price points, from affordable accessories for casual listeners to premium, limited-edition pieces that appeal to your most dedicated fans.

In order to do this effectively, aligning your merch strategy with data intelligence should not be overlooked. Rather than taking a blanket approach with generic items, micro-targeting your offerings based on data-driven insights is extremely important. This ensures you are providing merchandise that aligns with the preferences and desires of your specific fan base, thereby increasing the likelihood of sales and customer satisfaction.

Though merchandising might occasionally need an upfront financial investment (if you are selling offline — i.e. at tour dates), the return on investment can be much higher than traditional recorded music income.

As we continue riding the industry's tide of change, tangible products like merchandise are poised to remain a crucial part of an artist's revenue strategy. However, the change of pace also means it can be just as beneficial to invest in less tangible, but equally valuable, forms of capital. One of the most important investments an artist can make is in developing new skills that align with emerging technologies and industry trends.

Even with the possibilities of artificial intelligence, the core of music creation will likely always require some degree of human creativity and emotion. With that said, we cannot ignore the rapid advancement of such technology and how it is drastically reshaping things. But, it is crucial to not only be aware of these changes, but to actively position ourselves to thrive within them.

One area where AI has the potential to make significant inroads and potentially 'cut away' at revenue for creators is in sync licensing — the use of music in film, TV, and other media. AI-generated music is becoming increasingly sophisticated to the point where it is almost difficult to tell it apart from music created by real musicians. Of course, one of the pros of this for content and media producers is that it offers a cost-effective alternative and customized creations with much quicker turnarounds.

The prospects of this may seem threatening to some musicians, but for those who are forward-thinking, it also presents an opportunity.

Rather than viewing AI as competition, think about it as a tool to enhance your creative process, while expanding your skill set and income. Developing skills and proficiency in AI and machine learning, for example, is almost guaranteed to be a valuable asset for musicians now and in the future, granting the capability to combine artistry with new cutting-edge technology.

A skill set like this holds the power to give you enhanced insight on how to be more effective when working with AI music generation tools, making it possible to (for instance) quickly produce multiple variations of the same theme for a film score, giving directors more options to choose from. Or laying the foundation for a basic arrangement (much like sampling), freeing up your time to focus on the nuanced, emotional aspects of the composition that truly do require human insight.

Even as AI technology advances to the point where media producers can easily and theoretically instruct AI to create music for their projects themselves (without the need for outside assistance), the multifaceted nature of their projects demands their attention across various other critical areas, rendering it impractical in many cases for them to immerse themselves in the intricacies of the music supervision. Instead, they're more likely to seek out musicians and professionals who have mastered this technology.

Similar to how CEOs still value data analysts despite the availability of user-friendly data analysis software, media producers will likely continue to seek out professionals who can efficiently navigate the intersection of AI and human creativity.

Moreover, there is potential for artists to go from just using these tools to actively shaping their development. Musicians with thorough knowledge of both musical creativity and AI technology can partner (and have already been partnering) with tech companies to develop AI music tools, ensuring that the artistic perspective remains central in these advancements (a little more on that later).

This could even lead to new career paths, such as AI music consultants or AI-assisted composition specialists, keeping the perspective and expertise of human creatives in the mix.

Embracing these emerging technologies and developing related skills not only future-proofs your career, it also opens up new ways to generate capital to reinvest back into your artistic journey. Think about the favorable outcomes that could come with taking a short course in AI machine learning, then combining that new knowledge with your creativity and offering services in AI-assisted music production, developing and selling your own AI music tools, or consulting for tech companies looking to improve their music AI algorithms.

The possibilities are endless, and those who can bridge the gap between traditional musicianship and emerging technologies are most likely to be at the forefront of leading and innovating the next wave.

In the words of experimental and electronic music pioneer Brian Eno in the book 'A Year with Swollen Appendices', *"Whatever you now find weird, ugly, uncomfortable and nasty about a new medium will surely become its signature. CD distortion, the jitteriness of digital video, the crap sound of 8-bit — all of these will be cherished and emulated as soon as they can be avoided."* The same might just prove true for AI in music — what seems foreign or impersonal now may become a defining characteristic of the future.

Fundamentally, whether it is through AI or more traditional

sources, generating capital in music boils down to understanding the market and audience — just like any other industry. Music consumers want more than just songs — they seek experiences, intimacy, and, most importantly, community.

With revolutionary artificial intelligence on the rise and major labels investing significant amounts of capital into initiatives like the metaverse [81], more and more ways of monetizing music are on the horizon.

Regardless of how any of these strategies and others within the industry evolve, the fundamental principles of financial success will forever remain the same — much of which is rooted back in the strength of your community. It is why promoters will want to pay you, and why brands will want to partner with you. They all want access to that community you have taken the time to nurture. Therefore, being intentional about building, engaging, and developing one will enable you to always stay ahead of whatever comes next.

CONCLUSION:
A New Horizon

Revisiting a point made consistently throughout this book, **community** building requires a well-defined **brand strategy** that resonates with your audience. The next step is to then understand, cultivate, and expand your community, which involves utilizing and analyzing **data** to make informed decisions. Armed with this knowledge, and a foundational understanding of music **law**, artists can confidently determine and communicate their worth when approaching **deals**, with the goal of generating **capital** for sustainability and growth — allowing for a lasting music career.

What I hope to have achieved through these pages, beyond providing insight, is a mindset shift in how you as an artist approach navigating such a dynamic industry. Oftentimes, in the face of uncertainty, our instinct is to resist change or implement reactionary measures based on assumptions or fear. However, as went over in the previous chapter, the artists who will continue to thrive are those who view industry transformations through a lens of collaboration rather than competition.

As opposed to seeing innovations as dismantling traditional music monetization structures that they have to try and stop, progressive artists should instead identify pathways to collaborate with these advancements for their benefit.

Covered in the introduction, Roc Nation mogul Jay Z did not want to embrace the concept of iTunes at first (due to fans being able to access album tracks individually) [6], then he eventually launched his own digital music service with that very same core feature (which was later sold to Block, Inc.). In the same spirit, EMI executives were slow to embrace CDs when they first hit the market in the 80s, then years later the highest executive at the company (at the time) allegedly said they must *"embrace digital or die"* [9].

We see from these examples and others that the key to being a future-proof artist and/or entity in the music business is identifying easy access points to partner with emerging technologies and strategies.

Whether you're at the level of a Chance The Rapper and can strike a $500,000 deal with a streaming service like Apple Music to fund your next project [82], or if you're an aspiring artist using advanced AI technology for content creation and digital growth, there are ways we can all walk alongside evolution as opposed to standing on the sidelines and playing catch-up with it (as the music industry has done in previous eras).

The biggest challenge that comes with evolution is that it can be very disruptive, sometimes causing us to have to completely pivot in ways that are not always convenient. The silver lining however is that history has shown us that the greatest disruptions usually birth new opportunities. And with the industry being met with the realities of Web3 and AI technologies, we can expect more opportunities to arise. On the other hand, the impending impact of some of this new tech has been passionately debated, with some expressing concerns over ethics or it threatening human creativity.

But rather than reacting out of fear, some music companies are choosing partnerships. They recognize AI's inevitable infiltration can either diminish their relevance or catapult innovation, depending on the perspective and approach taken.

One example is Universal Music Group's partnership with YouTube to establish the YouTube Music AI Incubator, which we briefly mentioned earlier [53]. This collaboration, launched in August 2023, brought together talent and tech to explore innovations at the intersection of music and artificial intelligence. The goal of incubators like this is for big tech companies, such as YouTube, to responsibly develop new advancements in a way that augments creativity, productivity, and revenue for the people it serves.

For Universal, collaborating directly with a leading technology platform like YouTube (owned by Google) enables them to not only shape how artificial intelligence shows up in the music industry but also helps them to ensure the solutions it provides align with the needs and desires of music creatives. This way, there is no competition in the process of innovation, only progress through partnership. And that mindset shift is exactly the type of future-focused thinking required to remain at the forefront of such an unpredictable landscape.

Other labels like Sony Music Entertainment and Warner Music Group have been making similar preemptive moves by launching initiatives focused on identifying opportunities with emerging technologies. In 2023, Sony Music brought on former BPI CEO Geoff Taylor as VP of AI, in what Variety Magazine said may be "the first AI-specific senior executive role in the music industry" [83].

The year prior (2022), Warner Music Group invested in LifeScore Music — an AI-powered music production service, invented in part by the co-founder of Apple's Siri Tom Gruber [84].

The flip (and arguably more important) side to this is that as the music industry continues to move at breakneck speed, it can be tempting for artists and companies to jump on every new technological bandwagon as soon as they appear to be gaining some traction. But the key isn't to blindly chase every shiny AI or Web3 opportunity that comes knocking, but rather to strategically evaluate how these innovations jibe with your unique creative mojo and business objectives.

Take the cautionary tale of the music industry's short-lived romance with MiniDiscs (a CD, but smaller), which was being touted as 'the future of portable audio' when they first launched. It's the 90s era and Sony, the mastermind behind this tech, is pushing MiniDiscs harder than a bootleg DVD vendor at your local barbershop.

Fast forward some years and the MiniDisc was completely obsolete. The reality was that consumers were perfectly fine with their CDs and the new wave of digital downloads. The MiniDisc did not bring enough change to the listening experience for buyers to justify the spend.

In both the era of MiniDiscs and in today's landscape, the takeaway ought not be to just chase the new flavor, but to take a moment to understand how these technologies can authentically grow your community and amplify your career.

Be intentional about the collaborations you pursue (this includes both creative and professional/business collaborations), making sure they're in sync with your core values and goals. Focus on the partnerships that truly move the needle for your unique journey. Dive deep into a few key areas that resonate with your tribe, rather than spreading yourself thin trying to be everywhere and do everything at once.

Though as great as this advice might sound, when looking at all the intricacies of strategically building an engaged audience, crafting an intentional brand identity, properly leveraging data intelligence, structuring sustainable partnerships, and exploring new income streams, it can be very easy for emerging artists to feel overwhelmed and even discouraged; how exactly does one begin executing such a multidimensional approach?

Understandably at this junction, a common assumption is: "What I need now is a manager! Someone to assist me with a custom plan that incorporates all the above". Management can most definitely be an important addition down the line, but what a developing artist may instead need at this stage is more of a 'coach'.

Respected managers excel at creating and packaging opportunities for artists once fundamental pillars are firmly established. Conversely, coaches provide hands-on groundwork, tailoring career guidelines at any junction. Both play pivotal but distinct roles that uniquely support creatives, but music business coaching often specializes in the areas outlined in this book. They do this by offering more personalized guidance adapted to your current career status — while also training you in essential skills and systems designed to create long-term sustainability.

The value of coaches goes far beyond the world of music. World-class athletes, for example, have an entire team of experts like coaches, nutritionists, and psychologists supporting their development. Similarly, music creators can benefit from a support system that includes not only vocal and stagecoaches to help improve their performance but also music business coaches to help them enhance and develop their business acumen, strategy, and plan.

Just like a boxing trainer works with a fighter to develop their unique style, refine their technique, and build the stamina needed to go the distance, a music business coach helps an artist navigate the complex industry landscape, and cultivate the resilience required to weather its ups and downs.

A trainer would not just throw a boxer into the ring and hope for the best — they work with their clients to develop a strategic game plan tailored to their individual talents and goals. In a similar way, a music business coach is there to provide that same level of personalized support and guidance to artists. They help identify growth opportunities, offer honest feedback and constructive criticism, and equip creators with the tools and knowledge they need to succeed on their own terms.

A boxer wouldn't step into the ring without a trusted trainer in their corner. In the same way, an artist might not be tapping into their full potential without a coach by their side. Because when the bell rings and it's time to face the challenges of the game head-on, that preparation and support can make all the difference.

This parallel goes beyond athletes. Bringing it closer to home, you will often find professionals across the entertainment industry rely on coaches to help them level up and stay at the top of their game. From actors working with acting coaches to public speakers hiring speaking coaches to sharpen their delivery to dancers training with choreographers to perfect their moves — coaching is an essential part of success in various creative fields.

As musicians, it's easy to fall into the trap of thinking that you don't need that kind of support — and perhaps only want to tap into creative coaches that assist with things like your vocal and stage performances. But the reality is, in an industry where most artists are solely responsible for their entire business operation and not just the quality of their creativity, a coach to assist you in navigating the business of your music career can be just as, if not more, valuable as any other type of coach you might engage.

Additionally, coaching fees are generally more affordable and flexible than management commission rates. Rather than an open-ended percentage of income that could amount to tens or hundreds of thousands (or even millions) of dollars in the future, coaching packages tend to be structured as flat monthly retainers or per project — making specialized guidance accessible at any career level.

Before we started working together, one of my former coaching clients (who we'll call Amara) had already spent over $20,000 in one year on generic marketing services. Despite this significant financial investment, she still hadn't seen much traction or landed many tangible opportunities.

Through our initial evaluation, I discovered foundational elements like authentic brand messaging and audience engagement strategies had been overlooked. We realigned priorities to those critical basics, including refining her online presence and engagement strategy.

Just over four months later (and with a much more affordable spend), implementing this targeted approach led Amara to successfully fund her next music video and subsequent album through fan micro-donations using the system we established. This also allowed her to identify and connect with those who might be considered 'super fans' and begin nurturing those relationships.

The point being, sometimes what we assume we urgently need isn't always the precise solution for our current challenges.

Had 'Amara' continued throwing money into these generic marketing services without constructing her core priorities first, progress would probably have continued to stall.

Managers, lawyers, and even consultants can excel at constructing deals, but those opportunities must exist (or at least be feasible at your level) in the first place. That begins with coaching that equips emerging artists to organically nurture their own thriving ecosystem.

However, locking in a coach is not all it is going to take. Just like with success in any field, building that future-proof foundation starts with you. To that end, here are a few strategies you can start actioning right away:

1. **Redefine Community**: Don't just build a fan base, cultivate a movement. Use your music as a catalyst for the change you want to see. Engage with your audience on a deeper level, using storytelling and shared experiences to create a bond that goes beyond the music.
2. **Disrupt Your Brand**: Your brand isn't just a logo or a color scheme, it's a living, breathing entity that evolves with you. Don't be afraid to shake things up, to challenge the norms and expectations of your genre. Embrace those unconventional ideas and let authenticity be your guide.
3. **Hack the Algorithms:** Data is power, but it's not as much about the numbers and systems as it is about understanding the human behavior they reveal. Use data to dive into the psychology of your audience, using sentiment analysis and social listening to strategize around the desires and triggers that drive their actions. Use this knowledge to craft content and experiences that resonate on a visceral level.

4. **Align Agreements**: Deals aren't just about the money, they're about the long-term vision. Don't just sign on the dotted line, negotiate with your legacy in mind. Look for partners who share your values and are invested in your growth, not just your short-term gains (though these deals have their place, too). Furthermore, don't be afraid to walk away from a deal that doesn't align with you.
5. **Monetize Your Mission**: Your music isn't just a product, it ought to have a purpose. Look beyond the traditional revenue streams and find ways to monetize your artistry.
6. **Innovate Without Imitating**: Collaboration is key, but true innovation happens when you blaze your own trail. Don't just hop on the latest tech trend, find ways to use emerging tools to tell your story in a way that's never been done before.
7. **Master Your Mind**: Your mindset is one of your greatest assets as a creative. Invest in your mental health and emotional resilience, because (as we know) the road to success in music is often paved with setbacks and challenges. Cultivate a growth mindset, surrounding yourself with mentors and peers who push you to be your best self.
8. **Seek Mentorship**: Whether official or unofficial, find a coach or mentor. This should not be someone who tells you what steps to take, but someone who helps you uncover your own potential.
9. **Redefine Success**: Success isn't just about the accolades or the bank balance, it's also about the impact you make. Define your own metrics for success, based on your values and your vision. Celebrate the "small" wins *and* the "big" transformations, knowing that your journey is uniquely

your own.

10. **Create Your Own Lane**: The future isn't about fitting into the mold, it's about breaking it altogether (as we've seen time after time). You might start out as just a player in the game, but the goal ought to be to become one that changes the rules. Use your voice and creativity to shape your journey (and the industry as a result) into one that amplifies your values and vision.

In closing, it is my hope that through the examples, strategies, and perspectives shared within this book, you feel empowered, enlightened, and energized to fearlessly charge into the music industry's future. And remember, you do not have to go at this alone. A music business coach can help you receive more personalized support and guidance as you construct a solid foundation and pathway for your career.

The pages ahead remain unwritten. So as I put down my "pen" to close this book, it is time for you to take up yours and begin writing the next chapters. Because the next trailblazing artist could be you! Whether your path leads to winning your first Grammy Award, and/or carving out a sustainable and growing career in music on your own terms, remember that the key to longevity in this game is always remaining authentic while keeping your finger on the pulse of change.

But don't just take my word for it. Take action. Experiment. Make mistakes. Collaborate. Innovate. The only way to truly learn and grow in this business at any stage in your independent artist journey is by diving in headfirst and getting your hands dirty. And when the challenges come (and trust me, they will), remember that every obstacle is an opportunity in disguise. If I have done my job right here, you now have the blueprint to transform those opportunities into stepping stones that help future-proof your music career!

ENDNOTES

INTRODUCTION

1. Philips. "First Philips Cassette Recorder, 1963." Accessed January 1, 2019. https://www.philips.com/a-w/about/news/media-library/20190101-First-Philips-cassette-recorder-1963.html.

2. Philips. "Philips Compact Disc Player, 1982-1983." Accessed April 7, 2024. https://www.philips.com/a-w/about/news/media-library/20190101-Philips-Compact-Disc-player-1982-1983.html.

3. The Verge. "Rhapsody Rebrands as Napster." Published June 14, 2016. https://www.theverge.com/2016/6/14/11936974/rhapsody-rebrands-as-napster.

4. BBC Archive. "1983: The COMPACT DISC and EMI | Newsnight | Retro Tech." YouTube video, 5:14. March 5, 2024. https://youtu.be/lkyKNa3L0mY?si=bYBdPgZeKB0NDe0V.

5. Apple Newsroom. "iTunes Music Store Downloads Top 100 Million Songs." Published July 12, 2004. https://www.apple.com/newsroom/2004/07/12iTunes-Music-Store-Downloads-Top-100-Million-Songs.

6. Business Insider. "Jay-Z's New Album '4:44' and Its Release Strategy." Published 2017. https://www.businessinsider.com/jay-z-new-album-444-release-strategy-2017-6#2007-removing-american-gangster-from-itunes-1.

7. The Hustle. "The Economics of Spotify." Accessed April 7, 2024. https://thehustle.co/the-economics-of-spotify#:~:text=The%20biggest%20labels%2C%20including%20Warner,back%20to%20music%20rights%20holders.

8. Music Business Worldwide. "Music in the Metaverse: Redefining Music Rights in the Web3 World." Accessed April 7, 2024. https://www.musicbusinessworldwide.com/music-in-the-metaverse-redefining-music-rights-in-the-web3-world/.

9. Hypebot. "EMI's Hands: Embrace Digital or Die!" Published October 26, 2007. https://www.hypebot.com/hypebot/2007/10/emis-hands-dema.html.

10. Billboard. "RIAA 2023 Year-End Music Report: Revenue Up, Streaming and Vinyl Continue to Grow." Published February 10, 2024. https://www.billboard.com/business/business-news/riaa-2023-year-end-music-report-revenue-up-streaming-vinyl-grow-1235641188/.

CHAPTER 1

11. Kelsey Museum of Archaeology. "Music in Ancient Egypt." Accessed April 7, 2024. https://exhibitions.kelsey.lsa.umich.edu/galleries/Exhibits/MIRE/Introduction/AncientEgypt/AncientEgypt.html.

12. Time. "The World's First Recording of Computer-Generated Music – From Alan Turing's Computer." Published December 10, 2017. https://time.com/5084599/first-recorded-sound/.

13. Library of Congress. "Today in History - August 12: Edison Patents the Phonograph." Accessed April 7, 2024. https://www.loc.gov/item/today-in-history/august-12/#:~:text=to%20this%20page-,Mr.,recorded%20sound%20onto%20tinfoil%20cylinders.

14. Marr, Bernard. "Web3 and the Future of Music." Forbes, July 13, 2022. https://www.forbes.com/sites/bernardmarr/2022/07/13/web3-and-the-future-of-music/?sh=184b7ce82a29.

15. Stites & Harbison PLLC. "90's Flashback: Prince's Trademark Cautionary Tale." Accessed April 7, 2024. https://www.stites.com/resources/trademarkology/90s-flashback-princes-trademark-cautionary-tale/#:~:text=me%20at%20birth.-,Warner%20Bros.,related%20music%20marketed%20under%20Prir

16. Yahoo Finance Singapore. "Prince's 'Purple Rain' is Heading to Broadway." Published May 3, 2023. https://sg.finance.yahoo.com/news/prince-purple-rain-heading-broadway-043810693.html#:~:text=Purple%20Rain.%E2%80%9D%20The%20album%20sold%20over%2025,in%20the%20Billboard%20charts%2C%20winning%20Prince%20two.

17. Genius. "Nipsey Hussle – Last Time That I Checc'd Lyrics." Accessed April 7, 2024. https://genius.com/Nipsey-hussle-last-time-that-i-checcd-lyrics.

18. Complex. "Nipsey Hussle's 'Victory Lap' Debuts at No. 4 on Billboard 200 Albums Chart." Published March 4, 2018. https://www.complex.com/music/a/eric-skelton/nipsey-hussle-victory-lap-first-week-numbers-billboard.

19. The Guardian. "Inside Nipsey Hussle's Marathon Clothing Store: 'He Was a Real Revolutionary.'" Published February 6, 2022. https://www.theguardian.com/music/2022/feb/06/nipsey-hussle-the-marathon-clothing-store-los-angeles.

20. Vice. "LA's Black Food Entrepreneurs Remember Nipsey Hussle's Lasting Influence." Published April 2, 2019. https://www.vice.com/en/article/neaweq/las-black-food-entrepreneurs-remember-nipsey-hussles-lasting-influence.

21. Ingham, Tim. "Over 100,000 Tracks Are Now Being Uploaded to Spotify Every Day. That's Nearly One per Second." Music Business Worldwide, February 24, 2021. https://www.musicbusinessworldwide.com/over-60000-tracks-are-now-uploaded-to-spotify-daily-thats-nearly-one-per-second/.

22. Fortune. "You Can Now Interact With a Virtual Girlfriend on Snapchat Powered by GPT-4." Published May 9, 2023. https://fortune.com/2023/05/09/snapchat-influencer-launches-carynai-virtual-girlfriend-bot-openai-gpt4/.

23. Yale University Library. "A History of 78 RPM Recordings." Accessed April 7, 2024. https://web.library.yale.edu/cataloging/music/historyof78rpms.

24. The Guardian. "Columbia Records Introduces the First Vinyl LP, 1948." Published June 21, 2023. https://www.theguardian.com/music/2023/jun/21/columbia-records-introduce-first-vinyl-lp-1948.

25. Museum of Obsolete Media. "Compact Cassette." Accessed April 7, 2024. https://obsoletemedia.org/compact-cassette/.

26. *The Washington Post. "Shorter Songs Are Becoming Popular Again in the Streaming Era." Published March 30, 2024. https://www.washingtonpost.com/entertainment/interactive/2024/shorter-songs-again/.*

27. *Music Machinery. "The Skip: A New Metric to Measure Listener Engagement." Published May 2, 2014. https://musicmachinery.com/2014/05/02/the-skip/.*

28. *Luminate Data. "2023 Midyear Music Industry Report." Published June 2023. https://luminatedata.com/reports/midyear-music-industry-report-2023/.*

CHAPTER 2

29. *Ingham, Tim. "Over a Third of All Tracks on Streaming Services Get Fewer Than 100 Plays. But There's Still Hope…" Music Business Worldwide, February 1, 2023. https://www.musicbusinessworldwide.com/152-million-tracks-1000-plays-on-streaming-services/.*

30. *Today. "Adele's Last Album, '30,' Is Named After Her Age, She Says." Published October 15, 2021. https://www.today.com/popculture/music/30-adeles-last-album-named-age-s-says-rcna6109.*

31. Rolling Stone. "Ed Sheeran Announces New Album '-' (Subtract), Shares Emotional Single 'Eyes Closed.'" Published March 24, 2023. https://www.rollingstone.com/music/music-news/ed-sheeran-subtract-album-1234688629/.

32. Business Insider. "Verizon Just Dropped a Mysterious Super Bowl Commercial That Hints Beyoncé May Be Performing in Las Vegas in 2024." Published February 12, 2023. https://www.businessinsider.com/verizon-mysterious-super-bowl-commercial-hint-beyonce-appearance-las-vegas-2024-2.

33. Biography. "Michael Jackson - Growing Up in Gary, Indiana." Accessed April 7, 2024. https://www.biography.com/musicians/michael-jackson-growing-up-gary-indiana-jackson-5.

34. BET. "This Day in Black History: May 14, 1984." Published May 14, 2021. https://www.bet.com/article/3ftb7p/this-day-in-black-history-may-14-1984.

35. Michael Jackson Official Website. "Michael Jackson Spent His Days Off Tour Visiting the Sick in Hospitals." Accessed April 7, 2024. https://www.michaeljackson.com/news/michael-jackson-spent-his-days-off-tour-visiting-the-sick-in-hospitals/.

36. Michael Jackson Official Facebook Page. "Today in MJ History." Facebook post, September 14, 2020. https://www.facebook.com/michaeljackson/posts/pfbid0Ed1yCmQhmd7cZqsy1L6rw6Rh2uKLR-SAfnL6t4YUrskVyT44Bt4QFo2HqY1XpVKxUl?locale=zh_CN.

CHAPTER 3

37. Spotify. "What's New with Spotify Premium." Published October 18, 2018. https://newsroom.spotify.com/2018-10-18/whats-new-with-spotify-premium/.

38, Instagram. "Shedding More Light on How Instagram Works." Published August 11, 2021. https://about.instagram.com/blog/announcements/shedding-more-light-on-how-instagram-works.

39. Music Business Worldwide. "Spotify Acquired The Echo Nest for Just €50 Million." Published March 7, 2014. https://www.musicbusinessworldwide.com/spotify-acquired-echo-nest-just-e50m/.

40. Financial Times. "The Future of Music: The Economics of Streaming." Published January 21, 2015. https://www.ft.com/content/c77b7524-a15f-11e4-bd03-00144feab7de?siteedition=uk#axzz3PTv8LhlI.

41. IFPI. "Global Music Report 2024: State of the Industry." Published April 2024. https://ifpi-website-cms.s3.eu-west-2.amazonaws.com/IFPI_GMR_2024_State_of_the_Industry_db92a1c9c1.pdf.

42. New York Post. "BTS Confesses They Only Sang in Full English Due to the Pandemic." Published August 26, 2021. https://nypost.com/2021/08/26/bts-confess-they-only-sang-in-full-english-due-to-pandemic/.

43. Billboard. "BTS' 'Dynamite' Tops Hot 100 Chart." Published September 1, 2020. https://www.billboard.com/pro/bts-dynamite-tops-hot-100-chart/.

44. Billboard. "'Despacito' Loses Number One on Hot Latin Songs Chart to 'Mi Gente.'" Published October 26, 2017. https://www.billboard.com/pro/despacito-loses-number-one-hot-latin-songs-mi-gente/.

CHAPTER 4

45. Encyclopædia Britannica. "Statute of Anne." Accessed April 7, 2024.
https://www.britannica.com/topic/Statute-of-Anne.

46. United States Copyright Office. "Copyright Timeline: 18th Century." Accessed April 7, 2024. https://www.copyright.gov/timeline/timeline_18th_century.html#:~:text=On%20May%2031%2C%201790%2C%20the,period%20of%20another%20fourteen%20years.

47. Patry, William F. "Patry on Copyright." Accessed April 7, 2024. https://digital-law-online.info/patry/patry5.html.

48. SoundExchange. "Pre-1972 Sound Recordings: State and Common Law Copyright Terms." Accessed April 7, 2024. https://www.soundexchange.com/advocacy/pre-1972-copyright/.

49. World Intellectual Property Organization. "Copyright Law of Germany of 9 September 1965." Accessed April 7, 2024. https://wipolex-res.wipo.int/edocs/lexdocs/laws/en/de/de236en.pdf.

50. UK Parliament. "Copyright Act 1911." Accessed April 7, 2024. https://www.legislation.gov.uk/ukpga/Geo5/1-2/46/section/19/enacted.

51. AWAL. "The History of Record Deals, Told Through 11 Pivotal Artists." Accessed April 7, 2024. https://www.awal.com/blog/history-of-record-deals/.

52. Hendrickson, John. "Enrico Caruso: A Singer as Big as All Opera." The Washington Post, October 25, 2001. https://www.washington-post.com/archive/lifestyle/2001/10/25/enrico-caruso-a-singer-as-big-as-all-opera/1bedf843-1491-4881-8574-489a108b4a29/.

53. AWAL. "Signing a Record Deal, Decoded." Accessed April 7, 2024. https://www.awal.com/blog/signing-a-record-deal-decoded/#:~:text=It's%20standard%20for%20acts%20to,and%20the%20resources%20we%20provide.

54. Encyclopædia Britannica. "Advancements in Music Recording after World War II." Accessed April 7, 2024. https://www.britannica.com/topic/music-recording/Advancements-after-World-War-II.

55. Rolling Stone. "The British Invasion: From The Beatles to The Stones, the Sixties Belonged to Britain." Accessed April 7, 2024. https://www.rollingstone.com/feature/the-british-invasion-from-the-beatles-to-the-stones-the-sixties-belonged-to-britain-244870/.

56. United States Copyright Office. "The Digital Millennium Copyright Act of 1998." Accessed April 7, 2024. https://www.copyright.gov/legislation/dmca.pdf.

57. Gardner, Eriq. "Music Industry A-Listers Call on Congress to Reform Copyright Act." *The Hollywood Reporter*, June 29, 2016.
https://www.hollywoodreporter.com/business/business-news/music-industry-a-listers-call-879718/.

58. Roberts, Randall. "Rapper Russ on Success and Why It's 'Corny' to Focus on the Numbers: 'Everything Is Ego-Driven.'" *Los Angeles Times*, November 16, 2017.
https://www.latimes.com/entertainment/music/la-et-ms-russ-20171116-htmlstory.html.

59. American Bar Association. "Why Blockchain Smart Contracts and NFTs Are the Unmatched Solution for the Music Industry's Royalty Problem." Accessed April 7, 2024.
https://www.americanbar.org/groups/entertainment_sports/publications/entertainment-sports-lawyer/esl-40-01-winter-24/why-blockchain-smart-contracts-and-nfts-are-unmatched-solution-music-industrys-royalty-problem/.

60. Medium. "Smart Contracts for the Music Industry." Published October 9, 2017.
https://medium.com/humanizing-the-singularity/smart-contracts-for-the-music-industry-3e641f87cc7.

61. Music Ally. "Blockchain Music Streaming Startup Audius Raises $5.5m." Published August 9, 2018.
https://musically.com/2018/08/09/blockchain-music-streaming-startup-audius-raises-5-5m/.

62. CNBC. "Audius Lands TikTok Partnership and Its Token (AUDIO) Market Cap Surged." Published August 17, 2021. https://www.cnbc.com/2021/08/17/audius-lands-tiktok-partnership-and-its-token-audio-market-cap-surged.html.

63. Investopedia. "What Is a Blockchain?" Accessed April 7, 2024. https://www.investopedia.com/terms/b/blockchain.asp.

64. YouTube. "50 Cent Talks Business; New Independent Album, SMS Audio & Leaving Interscope Records." Video, 4:19. https://youtu.be/l96-y9PN5Lg?si=Oue1NLtEm9G7uIqY.

65. Techopedia. "Can the Blockchain Be Hacked?" Accessed April 7, 2024. https://www.techopedia.com/can-the-blockchain-be-hacked/2/33623.

66. IBM. "Smart Contracts: The Benefits of Smart Contracts." Accessed April 7, 2024. https://www.ibm.com/topics/smart-contracts.

67. Medium. "Smart Contracts for the Music Industry." Published October 9, 2017. https://medium.com/humanizing-the-singularity/smart-contracts-for-the-music-industry-3e641f87cc7.

68. YouTube Official Blog. "Partnering with the Music Industry on AI." Published August 16, 2023. https://blog.youtube/inside-youtube/partnering-with-the-music-industry-on-ai/.

CHAPTER 5

69. Nyongo, Sughnen. "What Beyoncé's Renaissance World Tour Said About The Economic Impact Of Black Women." Forbes, October 2, 2023. https://www.forbes.com/sites/sughnenyongo/2023/10/02/what-beyoncs-renaissance-world-tour-said-about-the-economic-impact-of-black-women/?sh=69a32a607fce.

70. Near Eastern Archaeology. "Entertainers in the Greco-Roman World: The View from Bacchias." Accessed April 7, 2024. https://www.jstor.org/stable/i361143.

71. Exchange Rate. "Greek Drachma." Accessed April 7, 2024. https://www.exchangerate.com/currency-information/greek-drachma.html#:~:text=However%2C%20some%20historians%20and%20economists,the%20daily%20wage%20for%20a.

72. Songtrust. "A Brief History of Music Publishing." Published August 16, 2018. https://blog.songtrust.com/brief-history-of-the-music-publishing.

73. Stassen, Murray. "Meet Sony Music's New Global Merch Arm: Ceremony of Roses." *Music Business Worldwide*, January 20, 2023. https://www.musicbusinessworldwide.com/meet-sony-musics-new-global-merch-arm-ceremony-of-roses123451/.

74. Rolling Stone. "Music's Crypto Boom: A Field Guide to the Web3 Goldrush." Published March 18, 2022. https://www.rollingstone.com/pro/features/music-crypto-blockchain-nfts-guide-1116327/.

75. Audius. "$AUDIO: The Audius Platform Token." Accessed April 7, 2024. https://docs.audius.org/learn/concepts/token/.

76. Kickstarter. "Amanda Palmer: The New RECORD, ART BOOK, and TOUR." Accessed April 7, 2024. https://www.kickstarter.com/projects/amandapalmer/amanda-palmer-the-new-record-art-book-and-tour.

77. Billboard. "Amanda Palmer Q&A: Why Pay-What-You-Want Is the Way Forward, and More." Published October 15, 2012. https://www.billboard.com/music/music-news/amanda-palmer-qa-why-pay-what-you-want-is-the-way-forward-and-more-1533797/.

78. Intercept Music. "Merchandise vs. Streaming: How Musicians Can Maximize Their Earnings." Accessed April 7, 2024. https://interceptmusic.com/Home/Blog?p=merchandise-vs-streaming-how-musicians.

79. Music Think Tank. "Merch Smarter: Unraveling 5 Common Mistakes Artists Make with Merch." Published September 26, 2019. https://musicthinktank.squarespace.com/blog/merch-smarter-unraveling-5-common-mistakes-artists-make-with.html.

80. Spotify for Artists. "Fan Study: Merchandise Insights for Musicians." Accessed April 7, 2024. https://fanstudy.byspotify.com/edition/merch.

81. Stassen, Murray. "Cher Makes Roblox Metaverse Debut with Warner Music Group and Gamefam." Music Business Worldwide, October 6, 2022. https://www.musicbusinessworldwide.com/cher-metaverse-debut-warner-music-gamefam-roblox12/.

CONCLUSION

6. Business Insider. "Jay-Z's New Album '4:44' and Its Release Strategy." Published 2017. https://www.businessinsider.com/jay-z-new-album-444-release-strategy-2017-6#2007-removing-american-gangster-from-itunes-1.

8. Hypebot. "EMI's Hands: Embrace Digital or Die!" Published October 26, 2007. https://www.hypebot.com/hypebot/2007/10/emis-hands-dema.html.

82. Robehmed, Natalie. "Chance The Rapper's Apple Deal Shows He's Taking Music Marketing Cues from Beyoncé and Drake." Forbes, March 17, 2017. https://www.forbes.com/sites/natalierobehmed/2017/03/17/chance-the-rapper-received-500000-for-his-apple-music-exclusive/?sh=7277faa34b16.

83. Variety. "Sony Music Appoints Geoff Taylor, Ex-BPI Boss, as Its First-Ever AI-Focused Senior Executive." Published August 22, 2023. https://variety.com/2023/music/news/sony-music-geoff-taylor-a-i-1235653059/.

84. Garner, George. "Warner Music Joins Investment Round in AI Music Tech Company LifeScore." Music Week, September 20, 2022. https://www.musicweek.com/digital/read/warner-music-joins-investment-round-in-ai-music-tech-company-lifescore/085357.

READY TO MAKE YOUR FIRST 'FUTURE-PROOF' DECISION?

Join a thriving community of independent artists who, like you, are committed to adapting, growing, and thriving in the ever-evolving music industry. As a member, you'll gain access to exclusive resources, insights, and services that are designed to help you navigate your artistic journey.

This is an opportunity to make your first "future-proof" decision and connect with like-minded creators building sustainable careers.

Connect today by **scanning the QR code below** (or visiting **themusicbiz.co**) and become part of a community that will taking you from just making music to making movements!

GET THE GEAR: OFFICIAL FUTURE-PROOF ARTIST MERCHANDISE

Represent your future-proof artist journey by grabbing exclusive merch from the official future-proof artist collection, featuring high quality gear that speaks to your commitment to evolving as an artist.

From apparel to accessories, there's something for *every* music creator!

Scan the QR code or visit fpamerch.com to explore the full collection and wear your ambition.

www.ingramcontent.com/pod-product-compliance
Lightning Source LLC
LaVergne TN
LVHW041610070526
838199LV00052B/3077